8/25/07

Dawn,
My sister-friend
be blessed on this
Journey
Love you
Irma

Still
on the
Journey

Still
on the
Journey

a collection of
spiritual meditations
and reflections

Jessica Kendall Ingram

Journey Press
Detroit, Michigan

STILL ON THE JOURNEY
*a collection of spiritual meditations
and reflections*

Copyright © 2000 by Jessica Kendall Ingram
Published by Journey Press

Cover Concept by Carol A. Bowie
Graphic Design by Elena Farmer

Library of Congress Cataloging-in-Publication Data
Ingram, Jessica Kendall.

Still on the Journey: a collections of spiritual meditations
and reflections

ISBN 0-9662962-1-4

Scriptures are from the New International Version,
the King James Version and the New King James Version of the Bible

Printed in the United States of America

Journey Press
A division of Journey Ministries
Jessica Kendall Ingram
19500 Stratford
Detroit, Michigan
313-342-2277

DEDICATED TO THE MEMORY
OF
RONALD DOUGLAS STEELE
AND
STEVEN MICHAEL KENDALL

*who in their dying
taught me much about living*

TABLE OF CONTENTS

ACKNOWLEDGMENTS

I have been able to stay on the journey of writing this book because of the ongoing support of some very kind and supportive people. They created an atmosphere that allowed me to work and gave me the assistance I so desperately needed during the months it took me to complete this book. With a profound sense of thanksgiving and gratitude I acknowledge those who helped me in making this journey:

Gregory Ingram, my husband, who was consistent in encouraging me to complete this book and who never asked me to stop working on it to attend to other tasks.

Jennifer, my daughter, who did not come into my study and disturb me but gave me the space I so desperately needed.

Sandra McLemore, for her computer knowledge and for being there to answer my every question.

Elena Farmer, for her expert knowledge of computers and graphic design.

John Bankston, Sarah Gibson and Dee Haynes, for proofreading my manuscript.

Carol A. Bowie, for her editorial expertise.

The members of Oak Grove African Methodist Episcopal Church — who read my reflections in the church bulletin and encouraged me to put them in another book.

INTRODUCTION

A few years ago my dear friend Renita Weems gave me a lovely large journal. Inside she had written these words: "Write until it hurts and then write until you are healed." Her words had a prophetic ring to them, for in the years to come I began to experience the kinds of hurts that were unfamiliar to me. The nature of my journey changed. I encountered new and different trials and tribulations. Tragedies occurred that weakened me. And I found myself struggling to gain the strength to keep on traveling.

The summer of 1998 was filled with the deaths of several members of my church. The one that had the deepest effect on me was the death of our church's Minister of Music, Ronald Douglas Steele. When Ron died I felt I could not continue the journey. He was more than an employee of the church; he was my friend, my spiritual partner, the one who made me laugh. He was my brother. Seeing him suffer from cancer was a draining experience for me. I watched him go from a strong vibrant man to one who was progressively weakened by a disease that rapidly caused his body to deteriorate. Although I was seeing his condition, I refused to believe that he would not be healed. So I encouraged the people of the church to fast and to pray. It seemed as though the more we did so, the sicker he became. I remember at one point saying to my husband, "If Ron dies I really don't know what I will do. I can't imagine coming to church on Sunday mornings and not seeing him sitting at that organ, singing and playing. I just don't know what I will do."

Prior to the summer of '98 I had taken pride in having a very disciplined and organized prayer life. My normal daily procedure was to begin each day by spending a minimum of one hour in quiet reflection, reading spiritual books, writing in my journal and praying. My spiritual journey was a good one: I stayed on the road, I knew my destination and I did what I thought it took to get there. However, I soon learned that we cannot always know the direction our lives will take. Events and circumstances happen that tend to change the nature of our journey. The wise person makes the necessary adjustment and keeps on traveling. The foolish person sits by the roadside lamenting, complaining and doing nothing. I decided to become a wise traveler.

I have been in the habit of keeping a journal since 1982. Recording my thoughts has kept me sane and has enabled me to face each day. Because my journals are my personal business, I write about what I want and in whatever way I choose. But in August 1998, I decided to share my journal writings with the members of my church by placing them in our weekly Sunday bulletin. It was risky business for me because it meant that they would see my weaknesses; they would read about my worries, my doubts, my fears, my issues and my concerns. However, because I believed the sharing of my personal reflections would provide healing for them as well as for me, I decided to expose myself.

On the following pages you will find thirty-one meditations and reflections that I wrote between

August 1998 and July 1999. Each week I wrote about whatever spiritual thoughts occupied my mind. Some of them reflected my struggles with trying to understand why God had allowed certain tragic events to occur in my life, as well as in the life of our church. Others focused on issues of life, such as making good decisions, deciding what to do with our past and learning to accept change. Sometimes I wrote specifically to church members, challenging them about their spiritual growth and assisting them in understanding what God is doing in their lives. I wrote the reflections hoping people would read them and then spend some quiet time meditating on them. I wanted people to gain strength for this journey called life and to keep traveling, no matter what happens.

I wrote because I was hurting and I kept writing because I wanted to be healed. In the process I learned that this life is not so much about reaching destinations as it is about the journey. Just when I thought I was healed (and was at the point of completing this book), my youngest brother, Steven Michael Kendall, died of cancer at the age of 48. I believe writing this book prepared me for the moment when I held him as he died. My writing has helped me to know that healing is possible. So I will continue to write (even as I hurt), knowing that I am still on the journey.

Still Traveling,
Jessica Kendall Ingram
March 4, 2000

HOW TO USE THIS BOOK

This book could probably be read in one or two sittings. However, I suggest that you not read it in that manner. It is not to be read in a rush or while you are on your way to do something else. This is a book of meditations and reflections. I wrote them for the purpose of the reader engaging herself or himself in serious spiritual contemplation. They contain deep insights that cannot be grasped or understood immediately. Therefore, you must carve out a specific time and space in your day when you can give your full attention to reading them. Slow down, sit down, be still, be quiet, ask for the presence of God to abide with you, and then begin to read.

There are thirty-one readings. I suggest you only read one a day. Thus, for a whole month you will have spent every day in quiet meditation and reflection. Commit yourself to spending a minimum of thirty minutes reading and reflecting on each entry. Be sure to have your Bible, a journal and a writing instrument available. Always read the full chapter for the Scriptures that are given. Because your thoughts will flow, take the time to write them in your journal. They will serve as a record of just how far you have traveled on your journey.

Finally, at the end of each chapter are questions. Answering these questions will help to make you accountable for what you have read. Answer each one as honestly as you can. In doing so, you will learn much about yourself and about God.

STILL ON THE JOURNEY

The angel of the Lord found Hagar
near a spring in the desert;
it was the spring that is
beside the road to Shur.
And he said, "Hagar, servant of Sarai,
where have you come from, and
where are you going?"
GENESIS 16:7–8 (NIV)

I suspect most of us have had experiences that sent us running to the desert. When we feel we can no longer gather the strength to face the uninvited, unwanted intrusions in our lives, our first inclination is to flee, to take off running somewhere away from all of the trouble and turmoil. We just want to tuck ourselves into a cocoon that will separate us from the pain and misery that seemingly refuses to leave us. Our strength has waned, our resistance is low, our heart is broken, our emotions are frayed and our spirit is weary. What choice do we have but to get away from it all? We were on our way, going somewhere, on the journey to our destiny. But now we have decided to turn back or at least to stop for awhile.

Hagar had fled to the desert. She no longer had the desire to continue her journey. She has been used by her master, Abram, and abused by her mistress, Sarai. Seeing no alternative to her present crisis, she took off running. Hagar found herself in the desert. I suspect the desert was not her intended destination. Actually, she did not know where she was going. Hagar simply wanted to remove herself from the presence of those who had violated her and had caused her much pain. Her status was that of a maidservant. Thus, she was in no position to challenge those who had charge of her life. She felt totally helpless. Nothing was left in her: no resolve, no strength, no will to fight, no desire to go on. For Hagar, the only alternative was to leave.

Have you ever thought about leaving? Did it ever occur to you to just pack up your bags and go somewhere, anywhere away from all of the confusion and chaos that seemed to come out of nowhere? Have you have thought about not staying on this journey called life?

There are experiences that happen to us that do strip us of our will to go on, our will to stay on the journey. Hagar's story is not foreign to us. It is indeed our story. We too have found ourselves victimized by the schemes of other people who are not concerned about our well-being. We have been in a position that does not allow us to do or say much about our circumstances. We have spent days and nights trying to figure out what happened. Our minds constantly linger on the situation, our thoughts are constantly interrupted by the memory of what took place. Where did it come from? Why did I not see it? Why couldn't I have done something to stop it? How can life be so unkind and so unfair? Unanswered questions and unchanged circumstances can sometimes lead us to a desert existence.

Hagar found herself in the desert, a lonely and dry place. It occurred to her that life no longer had any meaning; there was no hope for change and her journey had ended. Then something happened to Hagar in the desert. An angel found her, called her by name, spoke to her and asked two essential questions: "Where have you come from and where are you going?" It was a journey inquiry. They were questions that caused Hagar to stop, to reflect, to think and to make a life-changing decision. Sometimes we just need an angel to ask the right questions. The presence of the angel served as a reminder to Hagar that even in the desert God still remembered her. After some moments of dialogue Hagar got up and went back, knowing that her situation was still the same. The difference, however, was the change in her. Those moments with the angel in the desert caused her to realize that although she could not control the events that occurred in her life, she could control her response to them. This journey called life does not and will not always go according to our plans. So we must have an alternate strategy — and another one, and another one, and another one! A journey crisis does not have to change our journey destination. Hagar decided to go on, and so too must we.

God is looking for some Hagars. The two questions posed by the angel concerned her destination; they spoke to her journey. Would she allow the events of her life to keep her in the desert, to deter her from her divine destiny, or would she, in spite of it all, make the decision to keep traveling? Surely all of us must answer the same questions. Will we run to a dry place and stay, or will we listen to the voice of the angel and say, "No matter what comes my way, I'm still on the journey!"

QUESTIONS FOR THE JOURNEY

1. In Hagar's story, she was the victim. The story teller does not make mention of anything that Hagar did to cause her master and mistress to mistreat her. Have you ever found yourself in a situation where you were the victim? Explain.

2. In the case of Hagar, the angel came and ministered to her in the desert. Who has God sent to minister to you when you have found yourself hurt by the circumstances of life?

3. The angel asked Hagar two very important questions: "Where have you been and where are you going?" Think about them and then take some time to write your answers.

MISSING GOD

And, behold, the Lord passed by,
and a great and strong wind rent the mountains,
and brake in pieces the rocks before the Lord;
but the Lord was not in the wind:
and after the wind an earthquake;
but the Lord was not in the earthquake:
and after the earthquake a fire;
but the Lord was not in the fire:
and after the fire a still small voice.
I KINGS 19:11-12 (KJV)

I could not wait to go on vacation. Each day I was feeling the weight of the ministry more and more. I would wake up tired and go to bed tired. I had worked hard all year, meeting, administering, planning, organizing, preaching and teaching. To my surprise and dismay, the rest that I had anticipated did not come. In the past, I had always looked forward to the summer. The level of my work always tapered off and there was much less to do. So I usually had an opportunity to regroup and get ready for the beginning of another conference year, which in the African Methodist Episcopal Church is the twelve-month period from September to August. But the summer of '98 was different. It had not been a lighthearted, fancy-free, basking-in-the-sun experience. Instead there had been tragedy, sickness and death. It begin with the drowning of two of our congregations's precious teenage boys. It ended with the death of my most favorite person, our Minister of Music. I found myself in a peculiar and different place with God. This God I did not know. I was not familiar with this side of Him. And so I desperately needed to go on vacation, to rest and spend time restoring, reclaiming and renewing my relationship with God.

For the past six years, my family has always gone to a place by the ocean. It has become a requirement with me to have an ocean view. My daily routine was to get up in the morning, make my cup of coffee, gather my meditation materials, turn on some quiet music, sit on the balcony, gaze upon the great expanse of water and contemplate God. What a wonderful glorious time I would have. Looking at the ocean served as my reminder that God is indeed a great God. I had become dependent on this kind of experience. So to assure that I would have this magnificent view each year, I would always make my reservations early. The summer of '98 was no different. I had called in February and was told that the hotel could honor my request. In August, a week prior to our time of departure, I called the resort to confirm things. "Do we have an ocean view?" I asked. The answer was "Yes!" I was satisfied and ready to go. I was looking forward to my familiar experience with God.

When we arrived at our destination, I asked, "Do we have a nice place? Can I see the ocean?" The person behind the desk replied, "Your condo is wonderful, nice and new, but you have a view of the pond, not the ocean." My heart sank! I was so disappointed. As we unpacked our bags, I kept looking at that little pond and thinking to myself, "I can't find God in that little thing. I need my ocean!" Every morning for the next six days I got up, made my coffee, got my meditation material, sat on the porch and complained. "This is not what I wanted. I'm tired. I'm worn out. I need to feel the presence of God. I want my ocean view. I need my water. I need to experience God in the same way that I have in the past!" Every day, I ended my quiet time drained and empty. But on the seventh day something happened. As I was sitting on the porch, I looked around and began to notice that there were so many beautiful trees, that the grass was like an even sea of green, that flowers were blooming everywhere, and that there was a quiet presence. I began to cry. For six days I had missed God. I was looking for Him in the vastness of the ocean, but He was present in the smallness of a pond that was surrounded by His glory.

Too often we limit how God will manifest Himself in our lives based upon our past experiences with Him. To do so is to miss God. We, like Elijah, want to know God in our familiar places. And we want God to come to us in big, expansive ways. Not so. The summer of '98 taught me a valuable spiritual lesson: God can show up anywhere, at anytime, in any situation, if I simply look for Him. I try hard not to miss God's presence anymore.

QUESTIONS FOR THE JOURNEY

1. In the summer of '98 I needed to go to a familiar place where I could commune with God. I put things in order so that it could happen. I knew what had worked in the past. Where do you go, what do you do when you desperately need to experience the presence of God?

2. Sometimes we come to a worship service desperately needing to know that God is there, that God will speak a direct word to us. This is not an unreasonable expectation. After all, God's presence dwells in the tabernacle. But sometimes God does not show up for us. When this happens (and it will), what will you do to gain the spiritual strength to face the circumstances of your life?

3. For the next few days, begin to look for God in the "small ponds" that surround you. Revisit this reflection and write what you experienced.

4. Read the entire chapter of I Kings 19. What was it that caused Elijah to flee and hide in a cave? What has caused you to engage in the same kind of behavior?

THE ROAD LESS TRAVELED

*Enter through the narrow gate. For wide is the
gate and broad is the road that leads to
destruction, and many enter through it.
But small is the gate and narrow the road that
leads to life, and only a few find it.*
MATTHEW 7:13-14 (NIV)

A few years ago, M. Scott Peck, M.D., wrote a
book entitled, *The Road Less Traveled*. This well-read
work opened with these words: "Life is difficult." In
his next book, *Further Along the Road Less Traveled*,
Peck expands on this thought when he states, "Life is
complex. Each one of us must make (his/her) own
path through life. There are...no (set) formulas, no
easy answers. The right road for one (person) is the
wrong road for another...The journey of life is not
paved in blacktop; it is not brightly lit, and it has no
road signs. It is a rocky path through the wilderness."

There are those who go through life expecting to

find clear road signs that take them directly to their destination. But when they learn there are many detours and roadblocks along the way, many decide not to make the trip.

Life is indeed difficult. As we travel this road, as we make our journey, at any given time we may encounter pain, loss, disappointment, sorrow, disillusionment, fear, anxiety, problems, grief, betrayal or crisis. The old adage seems to be true: "We take one step forward and two backwards." Just when we think that we are making progress, moving forward and getting closer to our destination, some life-changing event happens that throws us off balance, causing us to lose our footing, or pushes us backward, draining us of our traveling strength. Few have the stamina to stay on the road and keep on traveling.

Jesus says that the road that leads to life is narrow and only a few find it. The landscape is filled with those who stand by the roadside watching with sad eyes as others continue on the journey. The only way to reach home is the hard way. There are no short-cuts. If we are going to make it, we must be determined. Determined to walk, even when we are in pain. Determined to keep going and face even our worst fears. Determined to conquer every obstacle and stumbling block. Determined to not grow weary and stop traveling. And, yes, because this road is traveled by only a few, we must be determined to keep going, even when friends will not go with us.

Life is difficult, but it is worth the effort. The journey is tedious, but you can make it. You have a traveling companion named Jesus, who will be your guide, even until the end. Stay on the road. You can make it!

QUESTIONS FOR THE JOURNEY

1. In two of his best-selling books, M. Scott Peck states that "life is difficult" and that "life is complex." Do you agree or disagree with these statements about the nature of life? Explain.

2. Jesus said that the road to life is narrow and only a few find it. If you have decided to travel on this road, it could mean that your friends will be few. Have any of your friends left you because of your decision to travel on the narrow road? What was your response?

3. What words would you use to describe the nature of your life's journey at this very moment?

4. When we travel we are usually trying to reach a specific destination. In our spiritual walk, we should also know where we are trying to go and then take the necessary steps to assure our arrival. What is your spiritual destination and how do you plan to get there?

WHEN YOU CAN'T PRAY

To everything there is a season,
and a time to every purpose under the heaven.
ECCLESIASTES 3:1(KJV)

Lately, I have given a great deal of thought to the purpose of seasons in our lives. We experience a season of great joy in our spiritual walk when we easily connect and commune with God. These times are called seasons of consolation. We really don't do anything to cause them; they just come. Then there are also seasons when we are unable to touch heaven, times when our most fervent prayers just seem to go up to the ceiling and bounce right back to us. We wonder what we are doing wrong. Are we not praying enough? Should we lengthen our prayer time? Are we not saying the right words? These times are called seasons of spiritual desolation. When we find ourselves in this most unusual place it is almost devastating to us, especially when we are going through some very difficult experiences. There are times when things happen to us that are so devastating that all we know to do is pray. However, if we are in a season of spiritual desolation, we find it hard to come before this God who seems so far away and seems not to be listening to us. The words to this song become a mockery to us:

> *"In seasons of distress and grief,*
> *My soul has often found relief,*
> *And oft escape the tempter's snare,*
> *By thy return, sweet hour of prayer."*

Our souls have not found relief. A cloud of despair seems to constantly hang over our heads. Our tears have become our meat day and night. The days come with a slow, dull beat. We present a public persona, which gives the impression that all is well. But our private reality is one of spiritual emptiness. Although we continue to come to worship and participate in the ministry of the church, we are really just going through the motions. Our prayer life is chaotic and we certainly are not experiencing a sweet hour of prayer. We can barely pray for a few minutes.

This becomes a season when we find ourselves asking the questions: "What purpose is this time in my life? Why does God seem so far away? If I can't pray, how will I make it?" I say to you, keep asking the questions. The answers will come, perhaps in a sermon or a song. Sometimes they will come through a Scripture. But often they will come from God's spirit within us. I know because I am there! These past few months have been my most difficult spiritual season. For weeks I could not pray. What I had asked of God, He did not do. I prayed for healing and it did not come. I prayed for life and instead He sent death's angel. This God I did not know. I stopped praying. But because I am a praying person, this season of prayerlessness felt strange. I needed to pray. When I began praying again, I found I did not have any words to express to God what I was experiencing. I would simply sit in God's presence in silence. Something different happened. My time with God became a season of learning. I learned that going through times of spiritual desolation is a normal part of our spiritual journey. It is during this time that though our words to God may be few, we learn that perhaps this is where God wants us to be: talking less and listening more. In those silent moments, I felt God's presence more than when I came to my prayer time with a multitude of words. Relief did eventually come to me, because the Holy Spirit was my intercessor.

Perhaps God allows these seasons of desolation to come in order for us to become totally dependent on Him. Indeed, to every season there is a purpose.

QUESTIONS FOR THE JOURNEY

1. Are you in a spiritual season of consolation or desolation? Describe what you are experiencing.

2. One of the spiritual principles I have learned is to never make a major decision when I am experiencing a season of desolation in my prayer life. Have you had the experience of making a major decision, even though you really had not heard from God? What were the consequences?

3. All of us have had times of spiritual desolation in our prayer experience. What has been your response to this kind of spiritual dilemma?

4. Have you ever thought about practicing silence in the presence of God? Are you trying to cultivate the ability to do more listening and less talking when you pray? Explain.

A REMEDY FOR THOSE WHO WORRY

Writing this reflection is risky business for me. Doing so makes me vulnerable, because I am allowing my weaknesses to be known. Most of us, especially ministers, want to present only our places of strength to others. I have learned, however, that I become strong and I help others when I am willing to recognize my own inadequacies, examine my unresolved issues, confess them to others and then submit them to God in prayer.

This time in my life is different. While I am sure of my relationship with God, I am not always sure of what God will do or what my response will be.

When my daughter, Jennifer was seven years old, she just blurted out these words: "You never know what God will do!" Wisdom comes out of the mouths of babes. We really never know what God will do with our lives. We are told that we must trust God with our future and that we should not worry about what will happen to us, nor take any thought about the concerns of tomorrow. We must walk by faith. We hear those words and some place inside of us wants them to become operative in our lives. A part of us wants to embrace that kind of Abraham-and-Sarah faith, where we pack up, leave and go to a new place, not knowing what will await us there. But if you are like me (and I think you are), there is a gap between hearing it, believing it and doing it. It is called worry.

Now, I did not want to admit to myself, to you or to God that I had begun to worry. I decided to look up the definition of worry in *Webster's* dictionary. I suspect I did so hoping that it would alleviate my worry about being a worrier. I seldom use the dictionary to define words I use in my preaching or teaching. Why use a secular instrument for spiritual insight? So I was confident that *Webster's* would relieve me of my concern. Surely none of the definitions would classify me as worrying about my future. The first meaning said, "To harass by tearing, biting or snapping, especially at the throat." That gave me relief! Certainly I did not engage in any of that kind of behavior. The next one said, "To assail with rough or aggressive attack or treatment." Relieved again! But then I read the third definition: "Mental distress or agitation resulting from concern usually for something impending or anticipated. *Webster's* had done exactly the opposite of what I wanted it to do. It confirmed that I had begun to worry.

My future is uncertain (as is yours). I do not know what God will do. I sense that God is in the process of making some major changes in my life. And I now confess that I worry about it. What will I do when my situation changes against my will? How will I respond? Will I adjust easily? After all, I am getting too old for all of these seasons of transition. I just want some things to be neatly arranged and to stay put for a long while. In asking these questions (almost daily), it occurred to me that although I don't tear or bite, don't attack and am not aggressive, I do worry!

As I wrote these words an amazing thing happened. An overwhelming sense of God's presence surrounded me and I felt at peace. I now realize that the remedy for worrying is to 1) admit that you do worry, 2) confess it to someone else, 3) admit it to God, 4) submit it to God and then 5) wait for God's peace to come.

QUESTIONS FOR THE JOURNEY

1. Take a few moments to think about the things in your life that cause you to worry. (Review the definition.) Without trying to make them sound presentable, write them down.

2. Are you willing to confess these worries to someone else? If your answer is no, write down why you are not able to do so. If your answer is yes, write the name of the person to whom you will tell your worries and when you will talk with them.

3. Find at least three Scriptures in the Bible that tell you what to do when you worry.

4. What steps will you take to go from being a worrier to being a person who embraces peace?

LIVING WITH UNANSWERED QUESTIONS

How long, O Lord must I call for help,
but you do not listen?
HABAKKUK 1:2 (NIV)

Habakkuk could not figure it out. He was a man of God, a prophet, one who honored God with his life, and encouraged his people to do the same. He had anticipated an orderly progression of events that would demonstrate God's love, protection and security. Instead, what he got was chaos, crises, calamities, attacks, destruction, disappointments, trials and tribulations. The intensity and longevity of the unwanted intrusions caused Habakkuk to ask some questions of God: "How long ... (will I ask you) for help, but you do not listen? Why do you tolerate wrong? O Lord, are you not from everlasting?"

Our responses to the challenges that confront us are really no different than Habakkuk's. We too question God when we come face-to-face with life-altering events. Before we can recover from one problem, we find ourselves surrounded by a multitude of new ones. Our natural response is to begin to ask God some questions: Why me? How did this happen? Why did you let it happen? How long will it last? When will it be over? How will I get through it? Despair sets in when we do not receive an answer. We desperately need to hear something from God. Nothing is seemingly worse than our needing to hear from God and all we get is silence. In addition to the frustration of hearing nothing, of receiving no answers, we struggle with the guilt we feel from having questioned God (because you know "they" say we shouldn't question God). There is an emptiness that lingers on in our souls. We find ourselves in a spiritual dilemma, first telling ourselves, "I have problems. I know God permitted them to happen and I want to understand why. I feel guilty about challenging God with my questions. To make matters worse, God will not answer me!" Then we ask ourselves, "How can I live with my troubles and unanswered questions at the same time?"

Allow me to respond to what you are experiencing. First, contrary to what some may say, it is alright to question God. It is a privilege that is given to those of us who are in relationship with Him. To do so doesn't mean that you doubt God. On the contrary, it says that you believe that God has the answer. Secondly, God's silence doesn't mean that God doesn't hear you, or that God is not concerned about your situation. It means that God is working on the answer, but you are not ready to receive it yet. (God's response to our questions does not always please us.

24

God's answer to Habakkuk, for example, was that things would get worse, not better. So in the meantime Habakkuk had to learn to live by faith.) Finally, Habakkuk stayed in dialogue with God, even though his situation did not change. Eventually, he moved from a posture of questioning to one of praying. Through prayer he came to understand that, although God's answer was not what he wanted to hear, although the crisis would still be present, and although the fig tree would not blossom, the crops would fail, the fields would not produce any food and there would not be any cattle in the stall, he could still rejoice.

When your questions are not answered, stay in dialogue with God. Stay in communion with Him. Don't stop praying. Soon and very soon you will learn that it is not so much about receiving an answer, as it is about receiving assurance. God will assure you that no matter what comes or does not come, His presence will be with you. When we come to understand this spiritual reality, we will find ourselves rejoicing anyhow. This is how we learn to live with the unanswered questions.

QUESTIONS FOR THE JOURNEY

1. What are some of the questions you have asked God for which you have not received an answer?

2. What has your response been when you have not gotten an answer from God?

3. Have you questioned God about a situation and received a totally different answer from what you expected?

4. What steps will you take to help yourself live in joyful coexistence with your unanswered questions?

CLINGING TO BROKEN PIECES

And the rest, some on boards,
and some on broken pieces of the ship.
And so it came to pass,
that they escaped all safe to land.
ACTS 27:44 (KJV)

John Mortimer, an English lawyer, wrote his autobiography and entitled it *Clinging to the Wreckage*. The title came to him one day when he was lunching with a gray-bearded sailor. He had asked the yachtsman if sailing on the English Channel was not a dangerous sport. "Not dangerous at all," said the man, "provided you don't learn to swim." Mortimer asked what he could mean by that. "When you're in a spot of trouble," he explained, "if you can swim, you try to strike out for the shore. You invariably drown. As I can't swim I cling to the wreckage and they send a helicopter out for me. That's my tip: If you ever find yourself in trouble, cling to the wreckage."

If the truth be told, we are all clinging to the wreckage, holding onto the broken pieces of our lives with all we've got. In the story of the Apostle Paul's shipwreck, the pieces of wreckage become the very life jackets and lifelines of salvation. "Some on broken pieces of the ship." Those who had been on the ship held on to what they could, in order to make it through the storm.

Often, all we have to cling to after we have experienced sudden storms are just bits and pieces of what used to be. The tragedy for many is that our view of brokenness does not allow us to see the new possibilities that can and will emerge, if we just hold on to the broken pieces. When we are shattered and fragmented, we tend to give up. So many have a naive perspective about this journey. Being broken does not mean that our life is over. It does mean that we must get a firm grip on what we have left and not let it go. Even those little pieces of hope can get us safely to shore.

Paul and those on the ship were on their way to do God's work when suddenly they faced a violent storm. The ship was broken into several pieces. It appeared that they would not reach their destination. But a centurion on the ship told those who could swim to go into the sea first and get to land. However, there were those who could not swim. They were told to hold on to the broken pieces. By doing so, they all made it safely to land. We should not be naive and think that because we are engaging in God's work that we will not encounter the sudden storms of this life. Actually, it is because we are doing the will of God that we find ourselves without notice being tossed to and fro on the turbulent waters of our existence. Whenever we find ourselves in these kinds of situations we must learn to listen to the captain of the ship and follow his or her instructions. Don't try to swim; just cling. For John Mortimer, swimming represented our trying to make it, based upon what we think we already know. Most of us when confronted with calamities initially think we know what to do, only to learn that our so-called knowledge is insufficient for what we are going through. Instead of trying to do it our way, we must learn to depend totally on God and in our broken state, cling tenaciously to God. It is called trust. If we trust God, God will give us all we need to make it to shore.

Sometimes all we have left is the wreckage of our lives. But if you just cling to what is left — broken hopes, broken dreams, broken visions, broken hearts — you too can make it in on broken pieces.

John Mortimer, *Clinging to the Wreckage: A Part of Life* (New Haven: Tickon and Fields, 1982).

QUESTIONS FOR THE JOURNEY

1. Have you ever been in the midst of doing God's work and suddenly experienced a storm that left you broken? Write about your experience.

2. What happened to you when you tried to swim, when you tried to use your own resources to solve the problem?

3. Can you recall any instructions God gave you when you were shipwrecked? Did you follow God's instructions or ignore them? Explain.

4. Have you really learned to fully trust God and to cling to Him? If not, explain why. If yes, explain how you learned to do so.

STRONG IN BROKEN PLACES

For when I am weak, then I am strong.
II Corinthians 12:10 (NIV)

Take a moment and look at the broken places in your life: broken hopes, broken dreams, broken promises, broken relationships, broken homes, broken body, broken heart. As you engage in this moment of reflection, you will find yourself experiencing some feelings of sadness, grief and possibly despair. When our lives are disrupted by brokenness, we feel vulnerable and weak. Vulnerable because we begin to see ourselves as having no defense against the next experience that will come along and break us. Weak because we had become attached to what we had; it defined us. It had given us a sense of comfort and security. We had grown accustomed to its presence and now we are having a great deal of difficulty adjusting to its absence. We begin to wonder if we will ever be strong again.

Lately, I have spent a great deal of time thinking about the purpose of brokenness. I have watched some vibrant and strong people reduced to tears in a maze of confusion. I've seen them struggling to maintain an outer appearance of being together, when inside they have been fragmented, broken into a thousand pieces. I have wondered, "How will they get through this? How will they come out of it? How will they make it?" As usual, God provided the answer to my never-ending quest to understand why he allows us to be broken. It came in a quote by the revered novelist Ernest Hemmingway, who said, "The world breaks everyone and afterward many are strong in the broken places."

Before we can be made strong, we must first be broken. Before a thing can be made, something must be broken. For example, before the house is built, the tree must be broken down. Before the foundation can be laid, the rocks must be blasted from their quarry bed. Before ripe grain can cover the field, the soil must be broken. Before God can use us, we must be broken. There is no making without breaking. The story is told about some exquisite porcelain that is made in a Chinese village. Especially striking were the urns. High as tables, wide as chairs, they were admired around the world for their strong form and delicate beauty. Legend has it that when each urn was finished there was one final step, a shattering moment. The artist would break the urn then put it back together with gold filigree. An ordinary urn was then transformed into a priceless work of art. What had seemed finished could not be until it had been broken.

When the Artist of our life allows us to be broken, we must understand that God does it to make us strong. Our strength does not come from the acquisition of things. It does not come from realizing the fulfillment of our desires, plans or goals. It does not come through relationships. It comes through the process of being broken. When we are broken and weak, we tend to draw closer to God. In so doing, we offer God our weaknesses and He turns them into strengths. Look back over your life and you will see that your broken places have made you a stronger person!

QUESTIONS FOR THE JOURNEY

1. All of us have experienced some form of broken-
    ness. Look at the following list and circle the
    areas that apply to you. Explain.

    broken dreams

    broken relationships

    broken heart

    broken home

    broken body

    broken spiritually

    broken promises

    broken hopes

2. When you experienced your time of brokenness,
    what was your response?

3. The Scriptures tell us that when we are weak we
    become strong. Have you become a stronger
    person as a result of going through an experience
    of being weak and broken? Explain.

LESSONS IN THE WINTER

It was you who set all the
boundaries of the earth;
you made the summer and winter.
PSALM 74:17 (NIV)

For years I did not look forward to the coming of winter. When the beauty of the autumn season would begin to fade away, a mild temporary depression would settle in my spirit as I thought about the days ahead. So quickly the weather turns cold, the hours of daylight are shortened and the evenings are long and dreary. The level of my productivity seems to decrease in the winter. The early sunset served as a catalyst to curtail my energy level. Winter with its freezing temperatures, snow storms and icy streets has not been my favorite time of the year. And what has made it so difficult for me is my frustration with

35

myself. I was never prepared for winter. At the end of each winter season, I would promise myself that I would be ready for the next one. And yet, each year I was in the same dilemma: winter coats not clean, mismatched gloves (I lose at least three pair every winter), no boots and no hat. As I would rush from my car to my destination, trying to shield myself from the cold, I would chide myself for my failure to be prepared for winter.

My posture has been that of passive endurance and just waiting for winter to end. I could not see any purpose in days that ended at 5 o'clock, or in those dismal evenings that come so quickly. Driving was a nightmare. Either I got stuck in the snow or my car never got warm until I reached my destination. Once I got home, I just wanted to snuggle up under a warm blanket, drink some tea and do nothing. Getting myself wrapped up to return to church for a meeting would take every ounce of determination I could muster. I just wanted winter to be over. But something happened and now I have a new understanding of the season.

The psalmist says it was God who made both summer and winter. The same God who gave us the sunshine of the summer, is the same God who gives us the cold of winter. It is God who establishes the boundaries and seasons of our life for a purpose. Winter can be a time of spiritual refreshing and renewal. Great things come in the wintertime. There is the time in which we pause to appreciate God's goodness as we gather for Thanksgiving. We wait with anticipation for the season of Advent, as we celebrate the birth of Christ. The New Year comes in the midst of winter and we are given the opportunity to move past the old and embrace the new. Just when we are getting weary of the lifeless trees, hazy days and bone-chilling cold, we come to the time of Lent, when we engage in serious reflection about our relationship with Jesus. Before we know it, we are celebrating our risen Savior and spring is upon us.

This year I am excited about winter. There are lessons that I must learn during this cold season in order to appreciate the sunshine and warmth of my next summer. It is God who ordains the winters of our existence, and God does so for his divine purpose. Rather than constantly complaining, we must learn to use this time to rest, to be still, to be quiet and to hear God's voice. We must have times, seasons in our lives when we cease our relentless activities and just wrap up in the presence of God and rest. Winter is a time of learning the lessons of trust. It is a time of knowing that the God who is with us when the flowers are blooming, the grass is green and the sun is shining, is the same God who is with us in the long dreary days of winter. This season is when we must learn to be prepared before the winters of our lives come. We cannot rush out at the onset of difficult times and try to get ready to deal with them. Just as I had to learn to have my hat, coat, gloves and boots ready before winter came, you too must learn to have yourselves spiritually prepared before the difficult days arrive in your lives.

Because I have learned the lessons, this winter has been a blessing to me. Much to my delight and surprise, I have experienced God in new and unexpected ways. I have learned that God will show up at any moment during any season. Yes, even in the winter of my existence, I have cause to celebrate!

QUESTIONS FOR THE JOURNEY

1. In this reflection I talk about winter as a season in our lives, a time when life changes and becomes long, dark and dreary. Describe a winter season in your life, a time when you may have experienced some degree of depression and you wanted to just go in your house, close the curtains and not come out for a long time.

2. "It was you who set all the boundaries of the earth: you made the summer and the winter" (Psalm 74:17, NIV). What is the psalmist saying to you in this Scripture?

3. What will you do to prepare for the winter seasons in your life?

A NEW PLACE IN GOD

Moses my servant is dead;
now therefore arise,
go over this Jordan,
thou, and all this people,
unto the land which I do give to them,
even to the children of Israel.
Every place that the sole of
your feet shall tread upon,
that have I given unto you,
as I said unto Moses.
JOSHUA 1:2-3 (KJV)

I had been trying to hear God's voice, to hear something from Him concerning the death of our Minister of Music, Ronald Douglas Steele. To tell you the truth, I could not believe that God had let Ron die. I was with him an hour before he passed and my heart was heavy as I watched him struggle to breath. I stared in disbelief at what had happened to his body; he was virtually skin and bones. Cancer is a terrible disease. Once it decides to take control of a person's body, it does so with the intent of reducing them to nothing.

Ron was so very special to me. When I came to

Oak Grove we immediately made a spiritual connection. Sometimes while I was sitting in the pulpit I would think about a song that I wanted to hear and without my saying anything to Ron, he would begin to play it. He was such a gifted musician, one who could play and sing anything. Not only did the members of the choir love and respect him, but the members of the church also had a special love for him. No one could have told me that God would not heal his body of cancer. We prayed and we fasted, but he died anyway.

In my confusion and despair I kept asking the question, "Lord, what would you have us to do now that your servant, Ron, is dead?" He *was* our music ministry. It was through his gifts that we had learned how to really praise God. Ron had taught us about praise and worship. He had the special ability to choose the right songs, songs that took us into the presence of God. After every special worship service we would leave saying, "That Ron has done it again!" What would we do without him? Finally, after several months of crying, grieving and hurting, I heard God's voice speak to me while I was ministering to the members of our Mass Choir. They had been trying to keep themselves together, but it seemed as though they were drowning in grief. They were singing the songs, but there was no longer a connection to the words. Our new minister of music was trying to inspire them, but they were not yet able to accept his presence in their lives. If they sang the old songs, it made them cry because precious memories of the good times they had had with Ron would begin to run through their minds. If the new minister of music tried to teach them new songs, they resented it and without verbalizing their thoughts, would sabotage learning them. I just kept

40

praying, asking God to help me to help them. After awhile I heard God speak and He said to tell them, "Ron, my servant, is dead. You are now my Joshuas. Listen carefully to the instructions I will give you. If you follow them, if you obey them, you will go to a new place in me. Trust me. I know what I am doing."

I am sure that when Moses died, Joshua asked God some questions concerning his future. He was accustomed to Moses being there for him and the people. Moses was the leader, the teacher, the guide. What would they do without Moses? He was the one who was leading them to a new place. I am also certain that Joshua spent many days and nights crying and trying to work his way through his grief. Because Joshua continued (even in his despair) to commune with God, he was able to hear the instructions that were given to him. God told Joshua it was time to go to a new place. Yes, he was close to Moses. Yes, he would miss him. Yes, he would continue to cry. But it was now time to cross over the Jordan.

As difficult as it was for me to accept Ron's death, I now see that it was a part of God's divine plan for moving my church to a new place in Him. Actually, the death of any of our loved ones can become an experience in seeking God in new ways. Grief is necessary; the tears must flow. But it is not until we come to the point of acceptance and celebration that we can hear God's voice speaking new and wonderful things to us!

QUESTIONS FOR THE JOURNEY

1. Have you experienced the death of someone who was very close to you? What were the circumstances of their dying? How did you respond?

2. What were your feelings toward God concerning their death?

3. Where are you in the grieving process? In denial? Confused? Overwhelmed? Depressed? Moving toward acceptance? Explain.

4. Have you come to a point of celebration and acceptance? If yes, explain. If no, why not?

5. What have you learned about God and death?

THE JOURNEY TO CHRISTMAS

I am afraid that we have taken on the spirit of Herod, rather than that of Mary and the shepherds. Advent should be a season of waiting in great anticipation for the birthing of the impossible in us. It should be a time when we spend moments pondering the meaning of saying "Yes!" to the spirit of Christ. It ought to include our quiet but determined journey toward Jesus, a journey where our destination concludes with the giving of ourselves to Him. We have gotten caught up in the mad rush to acquire things in order to have a "real Christmas." We have allowed this season to become more of a self-imposed burden than a blessing. We give expensive gifts, not so much because of love, but out of obligation. Finding the time to shop when our schedules are already overcrowded makes us irritable and most impatient. There are so many people pushing and shoving, sales people are tired and weary, our list is too long and our money is too short. We are shopping more for things for Christmas and enjoying it less. The days pass so quickly and we feel pressed to get ready for the holiday season by putting up decorations, wrapping gifts, purchasing food, making travel arrangements, mailing Christmas cards, etc. etc. and etc. Our journey toward December 25th does not include reflecting, waiting, pondering, seeking, praising, praying and worshipping. We have made this season a journey in chaos rather than one of peace.

There are twelve days of Christmas. Is it possible that we could spend those days really getting ready for Christmas? What if we shopped less and prayed more? What if we took a day just to spend time with God? What if we, like Mary, said "yes" to the impossible and sang a song of praise for the blessings that have yet to come? What if we, like the shepherds, were willing to watch for the Holy One? What if, like the wise men, we were willing to give of our best to Jesus? What if we humbled ourselves and fell down on our knees and worshipped Him? What if we said, "Be it done to me according to thy word"? I think the answer is this: Our journey would be different and we would experience the true meaning of Christmas.

QUESTIONS FOR THE JOURNEY

1. Reflect, briefly, on the last "expensive" gift you
    gave during the Christmas season. Was it given
    because of love or out of obligation? Expound on
    your answer.

2. The Christmas season certainly is viewed and
    celebrated differently as an adult than as a child.
    As a child we expect to receive gifts; as an adult
    we should want to give ourselves as a gift to God.
    How are you willing to offer yourself to God this
    Christmas?

3. More and more families each year make a con-
    certed effort to spend less money at Christmas,
    because they have decided to place more empha-
    sis on the spiritual aspects of the season. How is
    Christmas celebrated in your household?

WHEN I LEAVE MY CHAIR

*Those things, which ye have both learned,
and received, and heard, and seen in me, do;
and the God of peace shall be with you.*
PHILIPPIANS 4:9

I have a daily morning routine. Once I have
awakened, I prepare myself for my quiet time with
God. Everything is already in place: my tape player,
journal, Bible and books. After I make my one cup
of coffee, I head toward my chair in the living room.
I admit that it is a very comfortable chair. I like the
muted colors, the wide back and the thick cushions,
all of which makes it easy for me to relax. I settle
down, put my feet up and begin to quiet my spirit. I
write in my journal, read from my meditation books,
reflect on what I have read and pray. My goodness,
how I love sitting in my chair!

In my chair I read spiritual thoughts and my soul takes delight in them. I feel such a connection. It is as if the writers have taken up residence in my soul. They know what I need to hear. These writers have called my attention to the importance of learning to practice the presence of God. They have helped me in understanding that rest is essential to my journey. They have assisted me in seeing the need to take time for personal spiritual retreats so that I can remove the clutter from my life, thereby reviving my soul as I listen to the still small voice of God. I have learned that I must respect and embrace God's timing, and understand the significance of my spiritual seasons. I must learn to release the past and trust God for my future. Each day I must surrender my will to God.

When I am in my chair, God's presence is so near. I hear God's precious voice. I feel the brush of an angel's wings on my face. My soul is satisfied and I want to do what is right. I am focused, calm, serene and at peace. Everything is right when I am in my chair. If I could just stay there all day, I would be the best little Christian. The problem is I can't live my life sitting in my wonderful chair. I must face the marketplace of life each day. And oh, how quickly I sometimes forget the lessons I thought I had learned. I forget that when I was in my chair, I promised I would learn to quiet my spirit in the presence of chaos. I forget that I said I would speak with a calm voice to my family. (They often tell me that I need to go back to my chair!) I forget that God is in control and that my day will not always go according to my Franklin Planner. I forget that I said I would trust God for tomorrow, as I begin to fret and worry about my future.

My desire for the New Year is that I will become the same person when I am out of my chair, as I am when I am in it! When I leave my chair I want to still have a song in my heart, an urgency to do God's will, a determination to renew my soul, a commitment to remember who is in charge of my life, a patience with others and myself, a focus on what really matters, an inner peace in the face of chaos, and a trusting in God for today and tomorrow. When I leave my chair I want others to know that I have been with God.

Our moments of meditation, our times spent in quiet reflection, our minutes of reading God's word and our prayers mean nothing, if we do not inwardly and outwardly demonstrate in our daily walk that we have been with God. The true test of our spiritual maturity is not when we are sitting in the comfort of our chair, but when we leave it.

QUESTIONS FOR THE JOURNEY

1. What daily spiritual routine do you practice that allows you to quiet your spirit and experience the presence of God?

2. What do you experience inwardly when you take the time to read the Bible, meditate, write in your journal, read spiritual material and pray?

3. I alluded to how wonderful it is for me when I am in my chair but, how, when I leave it, I face the struggle of being faithful to what I have experienced in my quiet time. What struggles do you encounter when you leave your place of prayer and move into your day?

4. What will you do to develop a consistency between your prayer life and your daily reality?

TODAY I CHOOSE

... choose you this day ...
JOSHUA 24:15 (KJV)

Choices are what bring about change in us. To choose is to decide that you are no longer satisfied with coexisting with that which is not productive in your life. To choose is to take a look at what is, no matter how painful it might be to do so, and then to say I don't want to live with this anymore. A new year gives us new opportunities to decide, to choose to shed the old — old issues, old patterns, old resentments, old rivalries, old responses, old habits, old ugly ways and old sins. How is it that we look in the face of change and refuse to embrace it? Each day we live we are given the opportunity to redirect our

51

lives. We do so by the choices we make. Spiritual growth does not just happen; it occurs because we decide that we no longer want to be enslaved to our passions. It happens when we develop a thirst for more of God and less of ourselves. We cannot choose to have both God and ourselves.

Our present reality is a direct result of choices we have made. Some were good and some were not so good. Perhaps poor choices were made simply because we did not know any better. I often say that if people knew better they would do better. However, nothing is sadder than seeing a person who has been exposed to good decision-making data and yet refuses to use it. This is unfortunately the case with so many Christians. Each time you come to the place of worship, each time you hear or read the word of God, you are exposed to information that enables you to choose wisely. How is it that we can be in desperate need of change in our lives and yet refuse to do so? Why do we continue to cling to that which does not benefit us? Why do we meander around the pool of indecision and then complain constantly about how unfulfilled we are?

Perhaps it is because we refuse to gather the strength and discipline that is necessary for change. We have been seduced by the atmosphere of our time. There are so many ways of getting what we want without hard work and struggle. Not so with choosing. That takes something more than learning a new skill or pushing a button. It takes a willingness to engage in personal inner examination, admitting that something is not right, releasing the need to hold on to it, refusing to continue to allow it to be the master of our destiny and learning to be uncomfortable with existing in an in-between place. The decision must be made to render powerless the enemies that prevent us from making choices in our lives: procrastination, excuses, blaming others, waiting for others to decide for us, looking outside of ourselves for the answers and being down on ourselves. There is a different world that awaits us, if we choose.

Today I choose! Tomorrow may be too late! And so I choose to change my life and to live it in a way that fulfills what God had in mind for me even before I was conceived. No longer will I allow random events to curtail and stunt my growth. I am not a victim of chance and circumstance, and I can overcome through choice. God has given me decision-making skills and I will use them. I will make good, sound choices because I have a Source who will guide me in wise choice-making, the Holy Spirit. And I also have Jesus, who will strengthen me when I think about turning back. Today I choose. I choose life, hope, peace and calm. I choose dreams and visions and new realities. I choose to learn from my past and work toward a better future. I choose to love God with all my heart and soul, to love myself completely and to love my brothers and sisters. I choose to give of my very best to God each day. I choose to cherish each moment that I breathe. I choose this day to live!

QUESTIONS FOR THE JOURNEY

1. What choices have you avoided making? Explain why you've been "meandering around the pool of indecision."

2. Do you confer with God before making all decisions, or are you selective in the issues you take to the Lord in prayer before choosing which way to go? Explain.

3. What have been the consequences when your choices were made independent of direction from God?

4. Because self-love is a divine mandate, list three things you will choose to do this year to affirm that you love yourself.

WHEN LIFE CHANGES

Everything must change.
Nothing remains the same.
QUINCY JONES

Many of you probably remember a song that was written several years ago by Quincy Jones entitled, "Everything Must Change." I cannot recall all of the words, but the line that says "everything must change; nothing remains the same" stands out vividly in my mind. Life is indeed full of constant changes, ones that we want and rejoice about when they come and ones that are uninvited, unexpected and subsequently cause us great pain. Desired changes give cause for celebration; unanticipated ones give rise to anxiety, fear and worry. One of the biggest challenges we face is that of learning how to accept and adjust to change.

In many instances, change represents loss to us. Our life as we have known it is over, and we are confronted with facing and adjusting to a new reality. Everything within us resists it. We want our life to go back to the way it was. Grief is the visible manifestation of our response to change. We are sad, we cry, we have a loss of energy, we feel that we are in unfamiliar territory, we become angry, we ask questions and we wonder why it had to happen to us! Yet, somehow, I believe change is God's way of growing and maturing us.

One of the lessons we must learn in life is that possessions, circumstances and people are not placed in our lives forever. We must value and treasure them while they are a part of us, but when they are taken from us, we must learn how to grieve over them and then eventually release them. People who have a continuous downcast spirit are those who refuse to or simply don't know how to let go of that which no longer is. But then there are those who, even though they have lost their job (having been released after years of employment), or are confronted with serious health challenges, or have experienced the death of a loved one, are somehow able to gather the strength to stay on the journey of life with much joy. These are the ones who struggle through the losses and allow themselves to grieve them, but then come to the place of saying, "Though my life is different now and things have changed, I must go on!"

Very little in our life today is the same as it was yesterday. Changes have taken place. We cannot and should not expect our reality to stay the same. Change is inevitable! May I suggest to you that when life changes, you should also change. We should change from being so dependent on what was and accept what now is. We should change from allowing ourselves to be defined by our jobs, our relationships and even our health. We should change and realize we are not in control. We, therefore, must lean and depend totally on our God, who will see us through every change in life. We must change and celebrate our new reality, seek God for a new assignment, learn the lessons and wait in divine anticipation for the next change.

QUESTIONS FOR THE JOURNEY

1. What changes have taken place in your life that have given you great joy?

2. What unexpected changes have taken place in your life that have caused you great sorrow?

3. What was your response to the unwanted, the unexpected, and undesired changes?

4. Were you satisfied with your response? If so, why? If not, what did you learn about yourself from that response?

THIS THING IS FROM GOD

...this thing is from me.
I KINGS 12:24 (KJV)

I was reading my morning meditation from *Streams in the Desert* by Mrs. Charles Cowan, when I came across this Scripture: "... this thing is from God." Although I have read the twelfth chapter of I Kings several times, I never noticed this verse before. It seems as though God hides certain Scriptures from us until the time that we need them, or perhaps I should say until the time that we are ready to receive them in our spirit.

For several months now I have expressed to people through my teaching or my preaching that this season we are experiencing is not a season of spiritual warfare. This is not the devil doing these things to us. Rather, it is God permitting them to happen to us for a divine purpose. Actually, it would be so much easier if it were a "thing from the enemy." We would know how to handle that. How good we are at verbally binding up Satan, rebuking him, telling him (or her) that in the name of Jesus we have the victory. When we know that what we are going through is demonic, we get a spirit of determination to win the fight. Spiritual warfare we know. But what do you do when it is not the devil, but God? When we are struggling with Satan we go to God, but when the "thing" is from God, where do we go? How do we seek comfort and solace from the very One who is allowing us to experience this very difficult time in our life? How do we pray to the One who seemingly has decided that our prayers will go unnoticed for a while? It is very, very difficult! The ongoing temptation is to shrink away from God; to pray less, listen less, worship less, praise less and serve less. When we move into this posture, we miss the lessons that God wants us to learn and give the enemy a space in our spirit without him having to fight to be there.

There are situations that God permits to come into our lives. God gave Satan permission to disrupt Job's good life. Therefore, what happened to Job was a "thing" from God and not from Satan. Although Job went through a very difficult spiritual season, he stayed in dialogue with the One who had permitted such terrible "things" to happen to him. Sometimes God will permit a "thing" to remain with us, in spite of our most fervent prayers. This was the case with the Apostle Paul, who prayed three times for this "thing" to be taken away from him. The adversary had placed a thorn in his flesh to torment him, but

God permitted it to stay there for Paul to experience a greater measure of His grace. God tells him that His grace is sufficient and that His power is made perfect in weakness. In our theme text (I Kings 12:24), God gives a word to Rehoboam through Shemaiah, instructing him to tell Rehoboam not to fight the enemy, for this thing is from God.

When the thing that you are experiencing in your life is because God has permitted it to be so, find comfort in knowing that God has a vision of you in mind, but you can never become that person until you learn how to handle "things of divine adversity." Remember, all things do work together for our good, because God does know what is good for us!

QUESTIONS FOR THE JOURNEY

1. When you know that the thing you are going through is because of the tactics of Satan, what do you do to counteract his attacks?

2. Read the first chapter of Job and answer the following questions:
   a. What kind of man was Job?

   b. In the conversation between God and Satan, who introduced Job's name?

   c. As a result of this conversation, what kind of "things" happened to Job?

3. What "things" has God permitted you to experience?

4. How have you responded to God when God has permitted those "things" to happen in your life that you did not want or desire?

ANOTHER SIDE OF GOD

*Hezekiah turned his face to the wall
and prayed to the Lord.*
ISAIAH 38:2 (NIV)

The first weeks of February have become a difficult time for me. Seven years ago, my father died and although it has been some time, I find that I still experience some moments of sorrow. As much as I tell myself I will do it differently when the anniversary date of his death approaches, I find that I still cry as I remember so clearly all of the events that took place. My mind doesn't ask permission to remember; it simply does so on its own. Yes, I remember calling my father to wish him a happy seventieth birthday on Sunday, February 3, 1992. I think about the week that followed when we talked everyday.

My father, Finley Jesse Kendall, was not a minister. But he was extremely interested in studying the Bible. As a Sunday School teacher he would spend hours in preparation for his class. On occasion other churches asked him to come and teach on various spiritual matters. It came as no surprise to me that he had been asked to present a workshop on prayer for a church conference. Because he knew this was my area of ministry, he called to ask for some information. I promised that I would send the best of what I had immediately. To assure the arrival of the material, I sent it overnight from the post office. Everyday, I would call and ask if it had been delivered and the answer was "no." Finally, on Friday afternoon, my father told me not to worry about it. He said the Holy Spirit had told him what to say.

The next day I woke up thinking that I would call and wish him well, but decided that I would wait until the evening. But by evening my father had died. In the midst of teaching his lesson on prayer, just as he read the words from Psalm 91:1, "He that dwelleth in the secret place of the most High shall abide under the shadow of the Almighty," I am told that he looked up and gently slumped to the floor. I was at my church when the call came. I was in total shock. People were talking to me, but I could not hear what they were saying. I had just talked to my father a few hours ago and he was just fine. How could this be true? I remember getting on the plane that evening in total disbelief. I could not believe that my father was gone. But most of all I remember going to the funeral home to view his body. With tears streaming down my face, I turned to the wall and said, "God, this is a side of you that I do not know. I have known the God of life, now I must know the God of death." It has been a very hard thing to do, but in these past seven years, I have come to know and experience God in new ways.

There were dimensions of God that I did not know because I had no need to know them. Why would I need to experience the comfort of God, if I never really needed comforting? Why would I need to discover the ways of a God who can take away, when I had only known a God who gives? Why would I need to struggle to seek the God who is sometimes absent, when I had only known a God who was always present? Why would I know about the God who permits loved ones to die, when I had only experienced the God who had allowed my parents to live for all of these years? My father's death has given me the privilege of discovering "another side of God."

Our knowledge of God is directly related to the context of our everyday reality. In other words, we come to some kind of understanding of the nature of God based upon what is occurring in our lives. We come to know Him as the God who provides, only when we go through those times of lack. If we never experienced sickness, we would not know Him as the God who heals. If we did not have those times when the enemy fences us in, we wouldn't be able to boast about a God who delivers. If we did not have moments in which the tears stream down our face, how would we know that He is a God who wipes away the tears? If we never had a problem, how would we know that He is a problem-solver? There are aspects of the nature of God that we will never ascertain to, never have an awareness of, until we have gone through some things. So I am convinced that when God permits life-altering events to take place, He does so for the purpose of our coming to know something very special about Him.

Yes, I continue to cry when I think about my father. But I am also able to rejoice because of my new relationship with God. My father's death helped me to seek intimacy with God. When Finley Jesse Kendall was no longer there to provide me with encouragement, to tell me that I could do whatever I wanted to or to call me his special child, I learned that God could tell me those things and so much more.

I had not known this side of God, but now I know!

Questions for the Journey

1. If you have experienced either the long-term illness or sudden death of a loved one, write about the circumstances and share your response.

2. If you have experienced both forms of loss, compare and contrast your reaction to each.

3. When I walked into the funeral home and saw my father in that casket, it was the most frightening moment I have ever had. I felt so far from God, and yet in the subsequent years I have drawn so much closer to God. Have you responded to the death of a love one in this way? Explain.

4. What did you eventually learn about your relationship with God after experiencing the loss of someone you loved dearly?

JUST TO BE CLOSE TO HIM

Peter followed him at a distance,
right into the courtyard of the high priest.
There he sat with the guards and
warmed himself at the fire.
MARK 14:54 (NIV)

It is spiritually dangerous to follow Jesus from a distance. This posture doesn't necessarily happen immediately. It occurs through a series of acts that push us further and further away from being close to Jesus. Peter's distancing began in Mark 8:32, when he rebuked Jesus' words when Jesus told the disciples that He (Jesus) would have to suffer and be rejected. The distance between Jesus and Peter became greater when Peter fell asleep in the Garden of Gethsemane while Jesus was praying. Finally, when the men came to arrest Jesus, the Scriptures say that Peter followed him from "a distance." Shortly thereafter, Peter denied three times that he even knew Jesus!

In so many ways we are no different from Peter. We engage in acts that cause us to go further and further away from Christ. Peter apparently saw little harm in the words he uttered and the things he did in the presence of Jesus. But ultimately they drove him further and further away from Jesus. The Lenten Season is a time in which we must examine ourselves, to see where we have taken on the spirit of Peter. We are distancing ourselves further and further from Jesus every time we decide not to come to worship service on Sunday morning, or not to attend Bible study, or not to have our daily prayer time, or not to give our tithes, or not to use our gifts in God's service, or not to fast.

This Lenten Season our theme is "Just To Be Close To You." We are saying that it ought to be your desire to move into a new place in God, a new relationship, a new awareness, a new closeness. We ought to seek intimacy with him. This can only take place when we intentionally engage in spiritual acts. We cannot continue to satisfy the desires of our flesh and draw nigh unto God at the same time. We cannot continue to be spiritually undisciplined and expect to experience more of God's presence in our lives. Inconsistent, uncommitted, sometime, wishy-washy "Christians" are following Jesus from afar.

Peter had an approach-avoidance relationship with Jesus. He wanted (at least in words) to be close to him, but at the same time he avoided intimacy. Peter eventually found himself sitting in the court-yard, warming himself with the very people who would eventually crucify Christ. The scene is that of one who got comfortable sitting with the enemy. If we continue to ignore the call of God in our lives to become spiritually disciplined, we too will find ourselves keeping company with the adversary and denying that we know Jesus. This Lenten Season we must covenant to not get trapped in the Peter Syndrome. We must say that we want to get closer to Jesus, and then without hesitation do those spiritual acts that will draw us nigh unto him.

QUESTIONS FOR THE JOURNEY

1. Name the acts in which you have engaged that have caused you to follow Jesus from a distance.

2. In what ways do you have an approach-avoidance relationship with Jesus?

3. Define spiritual disciplines. How does practicing them help to draw you closer to Jesus?

DON'T GROW WEARY

Let us not become weary in doing good,
for at the proper time we will reap a harvest
if we do not give up.
GALATIANS 6:9 (NIV)

One day my teenage daughter, Jennifer, came into my study while I was working and began to randomly look through items on my bookshelf when she came across my journals. As she noticed how many I had (approximately twenty and this number did not include the ones in other areas of my house), she asked me, "Why in the world would you do so much writing?" She then took a journal off the shelf and read the first page. It so happened that it was my very first one. These are the words I had written on June 25, 1982, at 3:45 p.m.: "I purchased this book in order to keep a log of my spiritual thoughts. I commit myself to a disciplined spiritual life. It is my belief that some day my thoughts will be published and will help some sister in her spiritual climb ... I will image in my mind what I will to be. There is a fundamental difference between wishing and willing, the two are diametrically opposed to each other. I commit the center of my consent to willing."

For a moment I thought to myself, "My goodness, I have been keeping a journal, writing in it, having my morning meditation and quiet time for seventeen years and what real difference has it made in my life?" It was one of those days when I was growing tired of the hard work of spiritual growth, having to daily deny myself of the things I really want to have, constantly having to assess what I am doing and seeking God to show me how to do it better, wondering if I will ever feel that I have arrived where I am trying to go, and just needing something to give me the strength to go on.

Well, the very moment that these thoughts came to my mind, the Spirit of God spoke to me and clearly said, "Yes, your time spent in My presence has made a difference. Are you not now able to write down your spiritual thoughts? Have you not already published a book and this very moment you are working on another one? Are they not blessing other people? You can express what I want them to hear because you have spent much time listening to Me. Don't grow weary; you are getting ready to reap a harvest."

So often we miss our blessings because we give up too soon. We have been seduced by the atmosphere of our time into thinking that when we work on something, we should see results within a short period of time. We have transferred this way of thinking to our spiritual life. Subsequently, when we decide that we will pray daily, fast weekly and go to a Bible study, when we decide that we will practice spiritual disciplines, the truth of the matter is that we really do expect to see some tangible results real soon.

However, this is what really happens: When we don't get what we want, when we can't see any visible change or manifestation of anything different in our lives, we began to grow weary of the spiritual work and gradually slip away from it. It is a trick of the enemy. In God's economy, it takes consistent spiritual work and time for a visible difference to take place in our lives. What if after fifteen years of consistently writing in my journal, I had grown weary and stopped? There would be no book called *The Journey Inward* and I would not have written this one.

Yes, it has taken many years. But it has been worth it. Know this: It is only through your consistent, daily time with God that you will come to know what God's purpose and assignment are for you. I encourage you not to quit, no matter how tired you may become. Take some time to rest and renew your mind, body and spirit, and then go back to your assignment. I am witness number one to the spiritual principle of continuing to do good, no matter what it looks like. In the proper time, we will reap the harvest, if we do not give up!

QUESTIONS FOR THE JOURNEY

1. How aware are you of your purpose? Do you know your assignment? Explain. (If you do not, you must seek spiritual direction.)

2. What kind of problems, difficulties or challenges have you experienced in your commitment to doing the will of God in your life?

3. Have you ever stayed with your kingdom assignment, in spite of the obstacles or the attacks of the enemy on your work? Write about the harvest you reaped.

4. How do you recapture your spiritual vigor, when you find yourself growing weary of doing good works?

THE ROAD TO YOUR RISING

Arise, shine; for thy light is come,
and the glory of the Lord is risen upon thee.
ISAIAH 60:1 (KJV)

The road to your rising is not a smooth one. Your time to rise will not come until you have traveled the road of suffering, adversity, rejection and betrayal. If you back up or retreat when you encounter these challenges, you will never rise. Things do happen, events do occur that knock us down, and getting up takes more than just thinking about it. It takes a strong determination coupled with resolute actions. The poem "And Still I Rise" by Maya Angelou echoes this thought. No matter what happens, you must decide that you will get up!

The road that Jesus traveled to the Resurrection

reminds us of what happens before that glorious moment comes. Once Jesus lined up his will with God's, set his face toward Jerusalem and went about engaging in his Father's business, he placed himself in a position to be knocked down. Knocked down by those who resented His philosophy of change, by those who were intimidated by His power, by those who were jealous of the multitude that followed Him and by those who were envious of His self-confidence. As Jesus made his way to fulfill his divine destiny, there were always those who placed stumbling blocks in the road for the purpose of deterring Jesus and ultimately stopping Him. Jesus, however, already knew the kinds of obstacles he would face. They did not come as a surprise to Him. When he began His journey, He did so with a holy resolution, saying to Himself that nothing and no one would keep Him from fulfilling His purpose. Jesus clearly understood that before Easter Sunday morning, He would have to stop by Calvary.

If you have decided to make God's vision in your life real, to pursue your dreams, to accomplish your goals, to touch somebody's life, to find your place in God's kingdom, to use your gifts to make a difference and to do God's will, then you too must travel the same road as Jesus. Know this: Few will stand on the roadside cheering you on. As a matter of fact, do not be surprised if the people who are closest to you become the very ones who will turn from you. Remember that at Jesus' most crucial hour, all of the disciples left him. Do not be dismayed by those who constantly tell you that what you are doing is impossible. Do not allow the small mind-set of those who are not making the trip deter you. The journey to your rising is marked by people who really want to see you down. But remember: Only you can allow them to keep you there!

Knowing that you will rise is an awareness, an assurance that you must have, not at the end of the journey, but at the beginning. Once you decide to make the trip, you must immediately see your rising. "Arise, shine; for thy light has come, and the glory of the Lord is risen upon thee" are not words that are spoken to a people who have completed the journey. Instead, they are words of divine encouragement that were given to them at their darkest hour. We need words of inspiration not after we have gotten there, but while we are facing those obstacles on our journey. Our time of rising is not determined by a date marked on the calendar, but by our spiritual understanding of where we are going. You can be down at this very moment, but have rising on your mind. Nothing may be going right and it may look like you are going nowhere, but because you know who told you to make the journey, you already see yourself rising. Listen, do not allow what is happening in your life to fool you. Understand that your down position is only temporary. You must stay on the journey and your rising shall come!

QUESTIONS FOR THE JOURNEY

1. Most of us have been knocked down by some experience in our lives. Some blows are harder than others and we find it difficult, if not impossible, to get up, to rise. Write about your most painful experience of being knocked down.

2. When Jesus "set his face toward Jerusalem" it meant that no matter what happened to Him, He was determined to complete His mission on earth. Have you come to a place in your life where you have decided that no matter what happens, you are going to do God's will in your life? Explain.

3. Being knocked down is more than likely an experience that causes you to suffer. Paul says in Romans 5:3, "Not only so, but we ... rejoice in our sufferings, because ... suffering produces perseverance; perseverance, character; and character, hope." In other words, spiritual growth can take place in us as a result of our being knocked down. Explain how you have matured as a result of having one of these experiences.

DON'T SETTLE

But when they came to Haran,
they settled there.
GENESIS 11: 31 (NIV)

There I was, standing in front of the refrigerator talking to myself, hoping that no one would enter the kitchen and witness my temporary insanity. I had opened the freezer to retrieve my glass of ruby red grapefruit juice. It is my treat to myself in the evening. I had succeeded at convincing myself that it actually tasted real good—until this particular moment. Somehow, when I opened the door to the freezer compartment, the Häagen-Dazs butter pecan ice cream jumped out at me and actually began to talk to me, which is why I was talking to it, right? The Häagen-Dazs said to me, "You know how good

81

I taste, nice and rich and creamy, with lots of pecans scattered throughout my vanilla flavor. You've been real good during this Lenten Season, so you deserve this. Now think about it, what is the big deal about eating a little ice cream? How will that affect your spiritual journey? Nobody will know. And besides, God will forgive you!" Let me tell you that the temptation was great, but then I said to myself, "Don't do it. You are halfway there. If you have been able to make it this far, don't settle now. God will bless you in abundance if you go all the way to Easter Sunday morning."

Always when we make a decision to go with the Lord, temptations get in our way. They begin to talk to us and tell us that it is all right to stop now, that we have already done enough. These thoughts must have come to Abram's family as they were on their way from Ur of the Chaldeans to Canaan. Ur of the Chaldeans was the place they needed to leave. Canaan was the place to which God was directing them. Ur was the land of bareness. Canaan was the place of abundance. To get from Ur to Cannan was a struggle. Decisions had to be made. People had to be left behind. Travel was difficult. The journey was long and hard. Apparently the whole process became too much for some and they decided to settle in Haran. Haran is exactly halfway between Ur of the Chalderns and Canaan. There were those who died there, never making it to the land of promise. However, when Abram heard the voice of God telling him to not settle, to keep going, he obeyed that voice and went all the way to Cannon.

I suspect that you too have heard a voice speaking to you and telling you to settle. I suggest that you talk back to it and make it known that you have come too far to stop now. So often we miss the fullness of the blessings of God because we get side-tracked and distracted along the way. Once we decide to do that which is pleasing to God, to consecrate ourselves to Him, to practice the spiritual disciplines, to change our attitude, ways and habits, to turn from our sins, many, many voices will begin to talk to us and tempt us. Know this: The road to Canaan is not smooth. In order to make it to God's designated place of promise for our life, we must have a rugged determination to go all the way. Our weakest moments come when we are halfway there. This is when we begin to weaken and wonder if it is worth the effort. This is when the adversary begins to bombard us with all kinds of temptations. Don't be fooled. What God has in store for you is much more attractive than some Häagen-Dazs ice cream. The truth is though this dessert looks good and tastes good, it is actually bad for us. (This ice cream is on the list of foods that we should never eat. It is full of cholesterol.) That's the way temptation is. It looks real good and for a moment we might feel good when we succumb to it. But it should be on the list of things we never do.

There are full blessings that await us if we are willing to go all the way. During this Lenten Season decide that you will not settle.

QUESTIONS FOR THE JOURNEY

1. When you read this reflection, it may not be the Lenten Season. However, I am sure you have made some decisions concerning some sacrifices that you are willing to make in order to go to the place that God has shown you. What are these sacrifices?

2. Whenever we make a decision to go all the way with God, temptations get in our way. Mine was the ice cream that looked so good to me. What has been tempting you?

3. On this particular occasion, I did not give in to the temptation to settle for the ice cream. However, I must confess that there have been many times that I did yield to the temptation. When I did, I felt so disappointed in myself and so ashamed. How do you feel when you settle for doing less than what you told God you would do?

4. God told Abram to pack up and go to another place. This place was a land that would hold blessings for Abram and his family. Because Abram believed God, he was willing to go all the way and not settle. Where has God told you to go? How willing are you to go all the way? What would cause you to settle in Haran?

SETTLE DOWN

Be still, and know ...
PSALM 46:10 (NIV)

Have you noticed how tired most people look? Take a look around you and you will see faces that reflect pure and simple exhaustion. As I drive down the street and glance at the person in the car next to me, I seldom see persons who look relaxed and rejuvenated. They look as though they did not get enough sleep. I guess I fall into this category as well. Hardly a day passes without someone telling me just how tired I look. (Sometimes I think I look nice and refreshed until someone utters these words to me.) We look the way we do because of our long workdays. So many people have shared with me how they have gotten a promotion on their job, but it now means that they must work six days a week, 12 to 14 hours a day.

As I have conversations with other persons in ministry, without fail we talk about how our day never seems to end and no matter how much we accomplish, there is still so much more to do. With all that we are doing we ought to be tired, exhausted and worn out, but there is something different about this fatigue that we are experiencing. Back in the day, as they say, people worked long hard days, too. They did strenuous work in the cotton and tobacco fields, or worked in somebody's house or factory, engaging in hard manual labor. But somehow they did not seem to exude the same kind of weariness we see in ourselves today. I think the difference is that we are trying to do too many things at the same time and are finding that we are experiencing little if any pleasure in doing them, because we are too worn out to enjoy our accomplishments.

Our perpetual busyness, our insistence on always working, always doing something, always looking toward the next project or the next promotion, has resulted in our being tense, uptight and easily annoyed. We are often distracted, prone to respond in negative ways to the slightest irritation, lamenting about how much we are doing and becoming emo-tionally off balance and spiritually depleted. We need to get somewhere quiet and settle down!

The phrase "settle down" came about in the 1800s. It meant to set time apart for the quieting of one's nerves, centering oneself and becoming calm. When is the last time you decided to be still, to rest and to regroup? Somehow we think that our calling in life, that the measure of our success is to fill our days with much activity. We are addicted to the need to do something. Perhaps we don't want to settle down, because to do so, to sit and be quiet, to sit and think a whole thought through, to sit and reflect and process who we are, what we are doing and why we are doing it, is too threatening to us.

Being still and settling down forces us to get in touch with God's spirit in us. And I suspect we really don't want to hear what God has to say to us. When the spirit of God is able to speak to us, when we are able to hear God's voice, what God says to us, what God tell us to do and not to do, is so different from our own agenda. So we keep going, working, doing and complaining about how tired we are. To allow oneself to be carried away by a multitude of conflicting concerns, to surrender to too many demands, to commit oneself to too many projects, to want to help everyone in everything, is to succumb to a kind of inner violence. The frenzy of our activism neutralizes our work. It destroys our own inner capacity for peace. It ultimately destroys the fruitfulness of our work, because it kills the root of inner wisdom that makes work fruitful. Somehow we must learn how to be still and allow God's presence to fill us and renew our strength.

To settle down is to take a Sabbath rest from your labors. It is to restore the rhythm of life, to have a balance between work and rest. Sabbath time can be a revolutionary challenge to the violence of overwork, mindless accumulation, and the endless multiplication of desires, responsibilities, and accomplishments. Sabbath is a way of being in a time where we remember who we are, remember what we know, and taste the precious gifts of life. The Bible encourages us to "remember the Sabbath" and keep it holy. We are being told to remember to stop, to pull back, to slow our pace, to do less, and to cease our movement. God is telling us to reconnect with ourselves and with Him. Settling down, being still, honors the necessary wisdom of dormancy. If certain plant species, for example, do not lie dormant for the winter, they will not bear fruit in the spring. If this continues for more than a season, the plant begins to die. A period of rest in which nutrition and fertility most readily coalesce is not simply a human psychological convenience; it is a spiritual and biological necessity. A lack of dormancy produces confusion and erosion in the life force.

We, too, must have a period during which we lie fallow and restore our souls. In Sabbath time, in settling down, we remember to celebrate what is beautiful and sacred. When we do so, we find our way back to God and to ourselves. We become still and we experience the difference. Remember to settle down!

Questions for the Journey

1. Write down your activities for the past three days. Be sure to write everything.

2. In the past three days what have you done to settle down, to rest, to take some Sabbath time?

3. I stated that when we do not settle down, we do violence to ourselves. How do you interpret this statement in light of your own reality?

4. If you have not included rest in your daily or weekly schedule, what steps will you take in rearranging your schedule so that it will include definite periods of settling down?

STAYING IN JERUSALEM

On one occasion,
while he was eating with them,
he gave this command:
"Do not leave Jerusalem,
but wait for the gift my Father promised,
which you have hear me speak about."
ACTS 1:4 (NIV)

I wonder if the disciples inwardly resented being told to stay in Jerusalem until something happened to them. After all, Jerusalem was not a pleasant place for them. It was the city where they had abandoned Jesus. It was the city where everyone knew that they had been hand-picked to be his disciples, yet at His hour of greatest need, all of them had forsaken Him. In Jerusalem, they watched by the roadside as Jesus carried a heavy cross, and not one of them volunteered to help Him carry it. In Jerusalem, they witnessed the nails being hammered into His hands, the crown of thorns being placed on His head, and no

91

one tried to stop the soldiers from administering these inhumane acts. Even when they took Jesus down from the cross and placed him in a borrowed tomb, the disciples did not think about coming back with the spices to anoint His body. No, for them Jerusalem was a place of embarrassment and shame. Why were they being told to stay there? I am sure they wanted to move somewhere totally new and different, where no one knew them. Surely they wanted—and needed—a fresh start, to put their failures behind them and move on! But Jesus understood that until they stayed in the very place of their "mess ups" and faced their issues, they would never develop their purpose and move into their God-appointed and God-ordained destiny.

The disciples has issues. Issues. That's the word: issues. Like the disciples, we all have issues. And we all need to stay in our own Jerusalem and face them. This we do not want to do, which is why we are always trying to move on to something else. The tragedy is that until we do the necessary work of confronting our demons, we simply take them with us to the next experience, be it a new house, a new spouse, a new job or even a new church. Spiritual growth only comes to those who are willing to engage in the hard work of self-examination. Every now and then we need to just stay put and deal with our "ugly ways." All of this moving around, this never-ending activity in our lives, is simply a means of avoiding our issues. As long as we are accomplishing something externally, as long as we have a full agenda, as long as we have something to do, we don't have to really face ourselves.

If the disciples had not stayed in Jerusalem and examined themselves they would have never received the gift of the Holy Spirit. And they would not have become the powerful and anointed apostles of God's church. In Jerusalem, they faced who they really were: a group of men who were weak, fearful, inconsistent and powerless. They had to struggle with their issues of abandonment, desertion and betrayal. Staying in Jerusalem was the process that was necessary for their transformation.

Surely we too need to stay in our individual Jerusalem room until we understand why we have failed to be true followers of Jesus Christ. We must confess that we abandoned and deserted Jesus in so many ways. We too have been guilty of staying by the roadside, saying and doing nothing to help the cause of Christ. Are we not guilty of being more concerned about our personal safety and needs than we are about the cause of Christ? The Lenten Season in essence is about our learning to stay, to stay in a place where we can be honest with ourselves and God. These are the days when we must decrease our movement and position ourselves to hear from God. Acts of praying, meditation and fasting are the spiritual disciplines we must embrace in order to develop a new sense of who we can and should become.

The interesting reality is this: Although we have abandoned Jesus, He is still there for us. Now note this: In spite of all that the disciples had not done, Jesus did not leave them. He kept reappearing to them over and over again for a period of forty days. He kept speaking to them until finally he simply said, "Just stay here awhile and you will receive something wonderful." Because they stayed, the disciples received the gift of the Holy Spirit and they were empowered to accomplish the unusual. It is only when we learn to stay in Jerusalem, that we too will become those who are able to make a difference.

QUESTIONS FOR THE JOURNEY

1. In what ways have you deserted or abandoned Jesus Christ?

2. The disciples had been with Jesus for several years. They had spent time in His presence, listening to His teachings and ministering with Him. Yet, at His hour of greatest need, they were not there for Jesus. What factors do you think contributed to this kind of behavior?

3. If Jesus told you to stay in a place for a season, in order for you to engage in a time of personal, spiritual self-examination, what do you think you would learn about yourself?

4. When you come to the Lenten Season do you practice any of the spiritual disciplines such as fasting, increasing your prayer time, reading the Bible more or being more faithful in attendance of worship services? If your answer is yes, tell what spiritual benefits you receive from this experience. If your answer is no, tell what you will do to change your behavior during the next Lenten Season.

IN SEARCH OF MY OWN
GARDEN

*My mother's sons were angry with me
and made me take care of the vineyards;
my own vineyards I have neglected.*
SONG OF SONGS 1: 6 (NIV)

Self-neglect is not required. Somehow, we have been made to believe that we must always place our dreams and desires on the shelf of "not yet" and leave them there until we have taken care of everyone else's needs. While it sounds noble and good to do for others (and surely the Bible teaches us to do so), it is not good to ignore yourself in the process. Men and women are walking around with much built up resentment toward the very ones for whom they have sacrificed, given of themselves to, only to look around and discover how very little appreciation they receive. However, even more than that, they are

95

angry because, while they have helped others to move in their purpose and potential, they have yet to discover their own. Because each of us was created by God to fulfill our own destiny, our souls will never be satisfied until we do so. I have discovered that the people who are the most content with their lives are those who are working on their own God-given visions.

When my husband and I were looking for a home to purchase, I chose the one in which we now live basically because of the design of the backyard. Although it was small, it was obviously well cared for. The previous owner had taken the time to build a gazebo, lay a brick sidewalk, plant several different kinds of bushes, roses, day lilies and impatiens. During our first summer in our newly acquired home, I would often spend a significant amount of time sitting in my breakfast nook looking out at our lovely yard. I was enjoying someone else's work and declaring to myself that next year I would work on the yard myself. But the next year found me too busy to get in my garden to plant the flowers I loved. With each passing year, I got even more involved. There was always something to do, places to go and people to see. Summers would come and summers would go, but I never worked on my own garden. And while I was accomplishing much, preaching, teaching, organizing, planning, designing and implementing a variety of concepts, there was always this nagging thought in the back of my mind telling me that there was something more. Each time I entered my yard, I felt it. Every time I sat down to have a cup of coffee in the morning, it was there. I rationalized, I pushed it to the back of my mind, I pretended that I did not hear that little voice. I stopped looking out onto my yard in the mornings, thinking that it would

96

go away. It did not!

"It" will not go away until we submit to it. I cannot identify what it is for you. You know for yourself. You keep hearing that voice. You keep looking at "it," and yet keep passing it by. You keep finding excuses for not doing it. You keep covering it up by doing more of what you are already doing and never getting around to what God is showing you that you must do. At first I did not see the connection between working in my garden and experiencing more of what God had for me. In retrospect, I can see that it was not until I made up my mind to work on my own garden that I came into a new awareness of myself. Strange, isn't it, that when we engage in that which seemingly has nothing to do with what we have been working on, we discover more of our purpose and are energized to move in our destiny. When I began to work in my garden, I discovered this truth.

QUESTIONS FOR THE JOURNEY

1. In what ways have you neglected giving attention to your garden?

2. As difficult as it may be, answer these questions:
   a.) Do you neglect your own dreams in order to help others with theirs because you have a need to be needed? Explain.

   b.) What do you think will happen to the nature of your relationship with other persons if you decide to spend time working on your own needs?

3. How willing are you to engage in redefining your relationship with those persons to whom you have given so much of your time?

4. Be specific: What is the "it" for you? What is it that you want to see grow and develop in your life? What is it that you want to look out upon and be able to say, "God told me to do it, and I did"?

THE DILEMMA OF THE GIFTED

*While it's true that we are spiritual beings
with access to the same spiritual power
that created the cosmos,
we are enfleshed only by skins, not iron.
We're so easily bruised and scraped-especially
those of us who make it all seem easy.
Making it look easy is the hardest thing
in the world that we do.*
SARAH BAN BREATHNACH

I write today on behalf of that group of persons who have discovered their gifts and are using them. I write to express the thoughts of those persons who are walking in their God appointed destiny and have made the decision to focus their energy on the full realization of it. I write to encourage those who know that they have a purpose in this life and who with passionate resolve, are engaging in those experiences that help them to develop their potential. I write to heal those who have been hurt by the callous words spewed forth without editing from those whose small minds fail to comprehend the dilemma of the gifted.

Ironically, that which gives us our greatest joy can also be the source of our greatest pain. I once heard the pastor of a growing and thriving church express these feelings. He was the leader of a church that had grown by thousands. He was known as a spiritual giant. His name was spoken in all of the religious circles. His preaching style was imitated by many. So, surely, he was just expressing idle thoughts. Because I desperately needed to understand what he was saying, I asked him to explain his statement. On that day, I got a glimpse of what would meet me in the years to come. He said, "People see me as a great preacher. They see my gifts in operation. They see the fruit of my labor. They see the thousands of people who worship in my church. They see the many ministries I have created. And they hear my name everywhere. But what they don't see is the loneliness I experience. What they do not see is the profound sense of isolation. They do not know that I, too, hurt, that there are times when I need to be comforted, when I need a word of encouragement. They see my gifts, but they don't see me!"

Because we (yes, I put myself in the category of the gifted) make what we do look so easy, those around us fail to see that we, too, stand in need of encouragement, a kind word, a warm embrace, a note of thanks, a look of concern, an invitation to a place of rest. Yes, we are gifted. Yes, we believe in excellence in what we do. When we are given a task we do put our all into it. Yes, you can see the results of our labor. But just because we make it look easy doesn't mean that it is! It is not easy being different. It is not easy saying "no" to those things that do not promote your purpose, working long extended

100

hours, and seldom having moments where your mind is void of thinking, planning, organizing, analyzing and strategizing for the fulfillment of the next vision. It is not easy being gifted. And yet, if we would be accountable to God, we must be faithful and use the gifts that God has deposited in us, no matter how difficult it is to do so.

I have found ways to resolve the dilemma of the gifted. It is all about having the right perspective. First, I have come to understand that the gifts are not mine. They belong to God. They were not given to me for any selfish purpose. God gives gifts for the edification of the church, to establish His kingdom on earth. Anything that promotes righteousness will require sacrifice. If I am faithful in using my gifts, then I must constantly deny myself the pleasure of self-indulgence and give of myself willingly to God. This kind of understanding does not go unnoticed by God. Secondly, I have accepted what goes with the territory: rejection, criticism and exclusion. I have learned to count it all joy. Finally, I have learned to tell people what I need. In so doing, many have responded in some very kind, thoughtful and loving ways. Now I see my gifts as a blessing rather than a burden.

QUESTIONS FOR THE JOURNEY

1. Are you able to identify your spiritual gifts? (Read Romans 12 and II Corinthians 12.) What are they?

2. If you have been committed to using your gifts, what difficulties have you encountered?

3. What sacrifices have you made in order to be faithful in using your gifts?

4. I have learned to tell other people that sometimes I need words of affirmation, through a telephone call, a note or just a big hug. Write what you need from others. Begin to share your needs with them.

MAKE TODAY COUNT

*Teach us to number our days aright, that we
may gain a heart of wisdom.*
Psalm 90:12 (NIV)

I use to think that I had all the time in the world
to accomplish some things. Since I believed that I
had many days ahead of me, I felt no urgency to
make certain decisions, to accomplish certain goals
or to complete certain tasks. My unspoken philosophy for living was similar to that of Scarlet O'Hara
who, when confronted with a problem declared, " I
will think about that tomorrow!" In my twenties, I
believed that I had many tomorrows, and so I did not
deal with my emotional and spiritual issues.
Consequently, I was an emotional wreck and a spiritual disaster. Feelings of low self-esteem and insecu-

103

rity plagued me daily. I constantly compared myself to other women and I always concluded that something was wrong with me. I wasn't tall enough, I wasn't intelligent enough, I wasn't in the right profession, I didn't have enough class, I didn't wear the right clothes, I didn't know the right people—and the list goes on and on. Spiritual thoughts were not on my mind. My interest in God did not go beyond my asking God to answer my little selfish prayers. Once I got what I wanted, I moved on to the next item on my list.

Change, transformation, renewal, commitment, denial, discipline, sacrifice and holy living were not attributes that I embraced. Seeking divine guidance for my life, trying to discern my God-ordained purpose, working on a vision, walking in my destiny, making a difference or saying "yes" to the calling on my life never entered my mind. I was young and I had time! Now things have changed. Today, I turned fifty-two. I now realize that the days ahead are probably not as many as the days behind me. I cannot continue to wait until tomorrow to "think about it."

Being conscious of living each day to its fullest should not be limited to those of us who have grown older. Who really knows how many days are ahead of any of us? Daily we hear about those who leave this life at a young age. We were stunned by the death of John F. Kennedy, Jr. Who would have thought that such a young and vibrant man would not live to see his fortieth birthday? Tomorrow is not promised to any of us. We must make each day count. These are the thoughts that are expressed by the psalmist when he said, "Teach us to number our days." None of us knows the number of days we have left. We cannot afford to put off until tomorrow what must be done today. Each day of our life we must make decisions.

No more data is needed. We simply must stop wavering; go ahead and tackle the situation.

Today we must decide to make a difference, to say a kind word, to give a warm embrace, to lend a helping hand, to seek forgiveness and to forgive. Today we must work on our purpose. Our purpose is realized when we see each day as an opportunity to change some things in the earth realm.

Today we must see ourselves as God does: created in God's image, just a little lower than angels, a royal priesthood, a chosen generation. No longer can we wait to know who we are or to feel good about ourselves; it has to be today! These are our last days. This is not said in a morbid or pessimistic sense. It is to say this: Your best day is today! Today you can do God's will. Today you can change. Today you can make a difference. Today is your day of joy and peace. You must make today count!

QUESTIONS FOR THE JOURNEY

1. Write down your age. What do you know and understand spiritually that you did not know and understand ten years ago?

2. List three things that you have put off doing. Record the excuses (yes, that is what they are!) you have used for not accomplishing these goals.

3. We must learn to take life one day at a time. Name one action you will take today that will help in changing your life. Once you name it, commit to engaging in it daily until it becomes embedded in your mind and your spirit.

4. Find three Scriptures that will help you in choosing to engage in new and productive behavior each day.

NO MORE YESTERDAYS

But one thing I do:
Forgetting what is behind
and straining toward what is ahead,
I press on ...
PHILIPPIANS 3:13-14 (NIV)

For many of us, our yesterdays are filled with regrets of what we should have done, but have allowed our fears to keep us from even attempting to do. When we look at the days of our past, we see trails of unfinished business, footprints that led to nowhere, roads that were never traveled, dreams that were never pursued, visions that never became reality. Remembering is not always a pleasant experience. Yesterday was a time of embarrassment and shame. Our thinking about it produces feelings of guilt and pain. It becomes difficult for us to draw strength from our past in order to move into our future. We are stuck on what could have been. It is not the joys, the successes or the good times that stay with us. Instead, we are plagued by those experiences that tarnished us, colored our perspective on life, dimmed our view, blurred our vision, stymied our growth, arrested our development, turned us off, stripped us of our innocence, forced us to grow up too soon, or pushed us where we did not want to go. These things cause us to look at our yesterdays with tear-stained eyes, and bring about a rush of sadness that engulfs our entire being. How do we look at our yesterdays without being stuck on the pain? How do we keep from being controlled by what did or did not happen to us? How do we go on living without always looking back and thinking about what could have been? How do we release ourselves to move on with life? What shall we do with our yesterdays?

I confess to you that it took me years of struggling before I was able to answer these questions. Allow me to share with you the lessons I have learned about how to contend with my yesterdays:

l. Revisit the place of your pain for the last time. This time when you look at it, determine in your spirit that you will not go back to it again. Allow yourself to remember all that you can about it, when it happened, how it happened, who did it, what you felt, how you hurt and how you cried. Then say to yourself, "This is my last time. I will not allow myself to continue being held captive to this experience in my life. I confess that I may still cry about it, but I can cry and move on with my life at the same time."

2. Resolve old issues, whether they are someone else's that have affected you or your own. Unresolved issues become a weight that will hinder you, restrict your movement and get in the way of your forward progress. Avoid allowing someone else's issues to obstruct your view. Do not take ownership of them. You have enough of your own. Yes, you have issues. Admit that you do, stop living in denial, placing all the blame on someone else. Name your own demons and deal with them.

3. *Learn to let go of what you thought you would be and embrace what you are, while working on what you can still become.* A writer once said, "We must be willing to get rid of the life we've planned, to have the life that is waiting for us." All of us have had some ideas of what we wanted to do or become, ideas that have not come to past. It is counterproductive to keep rehearsing what you could have done. There is a life that awaits us that we will never experience until we let go of what we thought we would be. There is a new you standing in the shadows, waiting to emerge.

4. *Practice forgiveness.* Yes, forgive them and forgive yourself. Your inability to forget what happened, harboring ill-feelings, holding on to resentment, and nurturing bitterness and anger will only serve to keep you stuck in a place that obstructs your view of a different reality. Forgive them, even if they knew what they were doing to you. Unforgiveness blocks your blessings and hinders your relationship with God. We are told that if we do not forgive others, God cannot forgive us. Ask yourself this question: "Was this trespass against me worth my forfeiting my right to be forgiven by God?" I think not! Then you must forgive yourself. You really did not know any better. Recognize that you fell short of God's expectation of you, as well as your own. But do not continue to hold yourself hostage to it.

5. *Reinvent yourself.* You are more than the events of your past. Don't restrict yourself to what has been. There is much, much, much more to you.

Take the stuff of your yesterdays and recycle it into something new and wonderful.

You can do something with your yesterdays!

QUESTIONS FOR THE JOURNEY

1. Write about an experience in your past that was painful for you.

2. How has that experience affected the way you have lived your life?

3. Is there anyone in your past whom you have not been able to forgive? Why is it so difficult for you to forgive that person? What steps will you take to forgive him or her now?

4. Sometimes we have to let go of the dreams that never came to pass in our lives and begin to dream anew. What dream have you had to release? Do you have a new dream? What will you do to assure that it becomes a reality?

THE BLESSINGS OF SOLITUDE

*Solitude is a kind of boundary or
limit which enables us to disconnect
enough from our immediate surroundings
to discover what we ourselves
believe, know and value.*
KATHLEEN FISCHER

D o not confuse solitude with loneliness.
Solitude is what we need. Loneliness is what we fear.
By thinking that the two are the same, we miss the
blessings that come when we both seek and embrace
solitude.

Loneliness is what we avoid because it doesn't
make us feel very good. Who wants to be lonely?
When we are lonely we experience an assortment of
emotions (all within a few minutes). There is an
overwhelming sense of sadness, grief and even
despair. Feelings that accompany loneliness have
nothing to do with our being alone or by ourselves.

We can feel very lonely in the midst of a crowd. One might say that loneliness is a painful lack of connection with others. It is the sense that there are no others with whom we share the kind of understanding that lifts us out of isolation. Nobody knows the trouble we have seen. There is no one we can talk to who will understand our dilemma without our having to go through some long, drawn out explanation. We feel different. We think differently. We begin to believe that we really are different. Alienation and disconnection are the words that become our companion. Loneliness is painful; we fear it and try to allay its aching. When we don't know what to do with it, we become stuck in some place of nonproductiveness and find ourselves sinking more and more into the abyss of nothingness, doing nothing, thinking nothing, feeling nothing.

I repeat, do not confuse loneliness with solitude. If you do, you will never experience the profound spiritual growth that can happen when you learn the difference between the two. Do not allow the demons that surface during your seasons of loneliness to block the blessings that you can receive if you allow yourself to experience solitude. Embracing solitude is a decision. Loneliness enters our lives because we have become disconnected from our familiar surroundings, from people, places and things. We have allowed them to shape our identity and we feel lost when they are no longer with us. Solitude is a kind of boundary or limit that enables us to disconnect enough from our immediate surroundings long enough to discover what we believe, know and value. It is being alone for a divine purpose. It is a space or time apart, but one held and sustained by a sense of connection and peace with oneself and others. Solitude feels good because we are

114

reconnecting with our authentic self. We lose our true identity when we are always with others. We must have time alone where we can both discover our own inner depth and retain a sense of unity with others. The practice of solitude creates an atmosphere of silence, which we so desperately need. There are too many voices in our lives. Silence is a necessary condition for self-knowledge. When we decide to create spaces of solitude in our day, we are reducing the crowding of our heart and mind. In so doing, we are able to hear more clearly the voice of God and discover our own inner depths.

Do you not know that Jesus was clear on his mission and able to stay totally focused on it because He practiced solitude? Periodically, He would withdraw from the crowd, go into the desert and retreat to a quiet place. After He had this time alone, He was then able to continue His ministry journey. He did so with a clarity of His purpose and the power to fulfill His mission.

What we need is solitude. We should pursue it with a sense of urgency. We should take our lonely moments and turn them into experiences of solitude. We must create our own private spaces and withdraw from all of the noise and the activities that fill our days. When we do this, we will experience the blessings of solitude.

QUESTIONS FOR THE JOURNEY

1. What feelings do you experience when you are alone?

2. Explain the difference between loneliness and solitude.

3. Persons usually fear being alone because they are not comfortable with themselves. When we spend time by ourselves we are forced to face our demons. Have you avoided being alone because you were afraid of what you would learn about yourself? Explain.

4. Go somewhere that is peaceful and quiet, and stay there for several hours. Take a journal with you and write about your experience of solitude.

GOD KNOWS
WHAT IS BEST FOR US

*And we know that in all things God
works for the good of those who love him,
who have been called according to his purpose.*
ROMANS 8:28 (NIV)

A year ago I began to ask God many questions:
"Why are all of these trials and tribulations occurring
in my life at this time? What is the purpose? What
am I to learn from constantly being bombarded by
crisis after crisis? How could You allow this to happen? Why won't You answer my questions?"
Although God was not answering me in my appointed time, I knew that eventually He would. I expected God to do so during my time of prayer or when I
was releasing myself in total praise in a worship service. I just knew that God would answer me in the
midst of my reading the Scriptures or recording my

thoughts in my journal. God did eventually respond to me, but not in the way I expected. The words to the old hymn of the church are true: "God does move in mysterious ways!" One day, as I was entering the church, the security guard, Clanta Barnes, very politely asked if he could have a moment of my time. Since he never makes a request of this nature, I was more than willing to listen to him. Clanta shared with me a letter from his cousin, who is in prison, and said he thought I would be inspired by what his cousin had to say. Here is a portion of that letter.

I like the stationery Total Surrender. (The stationery was from a Women's Convocation given by our Ministry to Women in 1998.) It reminds me of this story. Let me share it with you. It goes like this: Once there was a great Prime Minister in India who had this kind of understanding. If a parent said to him, "My son has died," he would say, "Good, whatever God does is for the best." If a woman said to him, "My husband died," he would say, "Good, whatever God does is for the best." People hated him and thought that he was crazy and they were always thinking of ways to remove him from office.

One day the King was being shaved by his barber and happened to doze off. While cutting the King's nails, the barber accidentally cut off the tip of his finger. The Prime Minister's enemies thought this was their chance to get him. They rushed to him and said, "Prime Minister, the barber has cut off the King's finger." The Prime Minister said, "Good, whatever God does is for the best." The Prime Minister's enemies went to the

King and told him what the Prime Minister had said. The King called the Prime Minister into his presence and said, "You fool! You have been eating my food and living on my money and now have the nerve to say it is a good thing that my finger was cut off!" He ordered his men to put the Prime Minister in jail and to give him only water and bread to eat. "Now you'll see whether what God does is for the best," he said.

The Prime Minister sat locked up in his cell and calmly remembered God's name. He didn't get upset and when people would go to visit him and ask him, "How are you?" he would say, "Very good. God has put me here and it is good for me!"

A few days later, the King went off into the forest to hunt. On his way he was kidnapped by a group of men whose leader worshipped the goddess Kali. The group's leader needed to sacrifice an important person to the goddess. So he took the King to the temple as a sacrificial offering. The King's kidnappers examined his body thoroughly to see if his body was whole, because only one whose body was perfect could be sacrificed to the goddess. As they were examining him, they noticed his cut finger and said, "His body is impure, he is not worthy of the goddess." And so they let him go. Realizing that if his finger had not been cut off, he would be dead, he thought of what the Prime Minister had said: "Whatever God does is for the best." He realized that the Prime Minister was right!

The King returned to the castle and

immediately had the Prime Minister released from prison and told him what had happened and how it was good for him to have had his finger cut off. But he asked, "How was it good for you to be locked up in prison?" The Prime Minister replied, "If you had not locked me away in prison, I would have gone hunting with you and the group would have grabbed me, too. They released you because your finger was cut, but they would have sacrificed me because my body is whole. So you see, whatever God does is for the best!"

In an unexpected way, at an unexpected time, through unexpected persons, God answered my questions. God really does know what is best for us!

QUESTIONS FOR THE JOURNEY

1. When you have asked the "why" questions, how has God responded to you?

2. God used a person I least expected to answer my questions of Him. Have you ever had this kind of experience? Were you willing to receive what this unexpected messenger of God had to say to you?

3. What circumstances have you encountered in your life that initially did not feel so good to you or for you, but which you eventually realized God was using to work things out for your good?

GETTING OUT OF GOD'S WAY

Most of our lives bear so little fruit
because we are ever getting into God's way
with our own plans,
our own doings, our own fears.
M. BASIL PENNINGTON,
O.C.S.O.

A Catholic priest who once had the privilege of meeting Mother Teresa of Calcutta asked her this question: "Mother, could you give me a word of life to bring to my brothers at Spencer, my monastery in Massachusetts?" The priest states that Mother Teresa looked at him with those penetrating brown eyes (pools of love that invite you to rest in their quiet depths) and finally said slowly, with great emphasis,"Father, tell them to pray that I do not get in God's way." Mother Teresa was a wise person.

We are admonished in the Scriptures to acknowledge God in all our ways and then God will direct our path. The truth of the matter is that we have a tendency, a habit, of establishing our own path, and then of asking God to trail behind us. We really do try to lead God, only to become somewhat disappointed when God does not sanction the way in which we are going. If we are walking in front of God, then we are indeed in God's way. So often we don't have a clue about what God really wants for our lives because we are not still long enough, quiet long enough or contemplative long enough to hear what God is saying to us. We don't know the instructions for our journey.

I keep saying to myself, "What God has for me, it is for you me." The same applies to you. But we really don't know what God has for us. We stumble through this life coming up with all kinds of things we want to do. We devote a tremendous amount of effort to accomplish them, only to become extremely frustrated when they just don't happen. One of the spiritual writers, Father Pennington, has said that our lives bear so little fruit because we are ever getting into God's way with our own plans, our own doings and our own fears.

God really does have a plan for our lives. But we will never know it, if we do not spend quality time with God. When will we take seriously God's invitation to be still and know that He is God? We do need to sit in stillness and be before God, be with God, be in God. We do need to know in even deeper ways the truth of the Scripture that reminds us, "Apart from me you can do nothing"(John 15:5). It is a truth that we readily affirm, but rarely act on or live. How often do we plan a whole day, a week or even our lives without first consulting God? Yes, I understand the dilemma: God doesn't speak when we want Him to, or when He does speak we don't necessarily want to hear what He tells us to do. We have things to do, places to go and people to see! The urgency of our desires and wants supersedes our waiting to get directions from God. Yet, those who wait on the Lord are able to gain strength because, when they have the assurance that what they are doing is a part of God's plan for their lives, they receive supernatural power to get the job done. Knowing that you are operating in the path that God has chosen for you really does give you the wings of an eagle. Being uncertain of the direction of your journey only serves to sap you of your strength and keep you confused, meandering around in circles they lead nowhere. The ultimate purpose of this kind of spirit is to make you tired and weary so that you eventually just give up.

How easy it is today to get all of the information and directions we think we need from the Internet. It is just a matter of going into our computer system and bringing it up. Oh, how much time we save, now that so much information is accessible to us. Eighty million people are hooked up to the Internet. Eighty million people can have the information they need in a matter of seconds. I wonder how many of the eighty million are willing to wait patiently until they receive directions from God? You see, God is not on the "Net." The information that God has for our lives cannot be found at a web site. The fact is we need to slow down long enough to get to know who we really are, long enough to feel the brush of angels wings on our face, long enough to hear the sweet small voice of God speaking gently to us, long enough to listen to God's plan for our journey. The abundant life comes when we get out of God's way.

QUESTIONS FOR THE JOURNEY

1. Write down three plans you want to accomplish in the next six months.

   a.

   b.

   c.

2. What instructions have you received from God to accomplish these plans?

   a.

   b.

   c.

3. If you have not heard from God concerning your
   plans what will you do with them?

4. Write down three Scriptures that will help you to
   understand how to get out of God's way so that
   you can achieve the plans God has for you.

A SACRED PLACE

And he moved from there
to the mountain east of Bethel,
and he pitched his tent
with Bethel on the west
and Ai on the east;
there he built an altar to the Lord
and called on the name of the Lord.
GENESIS 12:8 (NKJV)

In her book *Sacred Dimensions of Women's Experience* Elizabeth Dodson Gray writes, "What hallows a space is what happens there. From the contours of our inner selves to the places in which we live, play, and work, we dwell in and move through spaces that take on meaning according to how we engage them. Sacred space is born of relationship, of care, of what we give and what we receive."

We all need sacred places, some appointed, designated location where we experience the presence of God, where we honor and recognize who God is, where we call on God's name. Such places don't just happen; we have to decide to create them. A room in your home, a cubicle on your job, a seat in your backyard, a trail where you walk, the car in which you ride, can become the place where you meet and honor God, if you decide to make it your altar. Sacred spaces are needed so that we might honor God and remember His promises to us.

My wing back chair, the ottoman and the mahogany round table in my living room have become the space where I meet God.

Many years ago, I came to the conclusion that beyond what I experienced in the sanctuary, I needed something more. My soul, my spirit could not wait until Sunday. No, I needed each day to connect with God. And so I decided to carve out a room in my house. It was a spiritual decision. I decided to go there each day. I decided to sit in my chair, to command my soul to be still, to contemplate God, to listen to God and to yield myself to God. My living room has become a Holy Place. There I feel the brush of angels wings on my face. There the thirsting in my soul is satisfied and my spirit is renewed. When I walk into the room, there is a difference. I feel it. I know it. I embrace it. It is calm, peaceful and serene. It is a sacred place. And because it is so, I honor it with my thoughts, my heart and my soul.

Somewhere east of Bethel (the house of God) and west of Ai (the heap of ruin), you will need a sacred space. Somewhere between the promise given and the promise fulfilled, you will need to create a location of remembrance. When we hear from God and then keep moving without stopping to honor what God has said, we may soon lose sight of the promise. After Abram received the promise of God, he had to travel to a new geographical location. What God had spoken to him would not be manifested where he was. He had to pack up his family and possessions and head toward the promise. What Abram clearly understood was the importance of staying connected to God. Synagogues, the tent of meeting, the tabernacle, places of worship were not yet established. Abram decided to built his own altar. He created his own sacred space. And there he called on the name of the Lord.

Between Bethel and Ai you will need to have somewhere to settle your spirit, somewhere to renew your strength. somewhere to restore your soul and to put on your wings. When you leave Bethel, the house of God, you will encounter Ai, the place of ruin. Trust me, you will need a sacred place.

QUESTIONS FOR THE JOURNEY

1. Where do you go when you stand in need of a sacred place? What makes this place a space where you can meet God?

2. Do you have a place in your home where you can be alone? If yes, describe it. If no, why not?

3. If you have not created a sacred place in your home, what steps will you take to create one?

4. In my sacred place I have my Bible, my journal and meditation books. I usually have my tape player available to listen to some quiet music. Sometimes I light a candle. Every now and then I will place fresh flowers on the table. Of late, I have been making a fire in our fireplace. All of this helps to establish a kind of quiet, sacred atmosphere. What items have meaning for you that you will put in your sacred place?

A LESSON IN FORGIVENESS

… forgive us our debts,
as we forgive our debtors.
MATTHEW 6:12 (KJV)

I could not believe what my ears had just heard. Was he really sitting in my sacred office saying these things to me? Did he really open his mouth and utter those words in my presence? I wasn't expecting it. I was caught off guard. I didn't anticipate its coming. I felt wounded, hurt and violated. But mostly I was angry. How could he talk like that to me after all I had done for him? (Please note: The him is not my husband.) He left me no options; the obvious action for me to take after such blatant betrayal was to stop being so kind to him. Does not the Bible say, "Don't caste your pearls before swine"? My plan to demonstrate to him just how wrong he had been included speaking to him, but making sure I said as few words as possible. I must also let him know that, because I am so spiritual, I would certainly forgive him, but he must also be told that our relationship would never be the same.

Shortly after this experience happened, I realized that I had never preached a sermon on forgiveness. Nor had I written a reflection on the subject. Perhaps I had not done so because those of us who minister the word tend to preach, teach and write about those areas that we have struggled with and overcome. Forgiveness had never been my struggle, or so I thought! Actually, I took pride in talking about all the people in the church I had been able to forgive. There were those whom I had trusted and who eventually betrayed me; those who had slandered my name and lied on me; those who look the other way when they see me coming, and those who don't like me because they just don't like me. Yes, I was confident of my ability to forgive. Apparently I was mistaken. I had been fooling myself, for I am telling you, there was something about this one that would not allow me to melt down my heart so easily.

For weeks now, God has been urging me to write about forgiveness, and I have been dancing all around it. How much more of myself do I need to expose? A few weeks after this incident happened, one of our ministers preached a powerful sermon on forgiveness. I thought, "Good. Now I don't have to write about it in my reflections." But the Lord said, "Not so. Write, for the truth will set you and others free." I did forgive the person. And what is so utterly amazing to me is the new kind of love I now have for him. This time I really did take it to God in prayer, and I asked God in total sincerity to help me love him in the way that God loves me, with all of my faults, frailties and failings. I prayed for the ability to love him with a godly love. As a result of this kind of praying, some interesting revelations came to me, and significant changes took place in me. First, I experienced a deeper and more profound awareness of how much God really loves me. After all, how many times and in how many ways had I done things to betray God and, yet, he has never withdrawn his love from me? God has never decided to go the other way. Next, I discovered that extending that kind of love to someone who had trespassed against me was more important than keeping score of his wrongs, being angry, not speaking or feeling so self-right-eous. It was and is a liberating experience.

Our relationship is not the same. It is the kind that has withstood the strain of change. It is more mature, not built on false expectations but on a relationship that operates out of an awareness that from time to time our faults will surface. However, when that happens (and it probably will again), I now know that it is possible to forgive. And how many times must I forgive him? Over and over and over again, just as God keeps forgiving me, over and over and over again. It is a lesson in forgiveness.

QUESTIONS FOR THE JOURNEY

1. Is there anyone you have not forgiven for trespassing against you? If your answer is yes, write why it is so difficult for you to forgive that person.

2. What steps will you take to forgive that person?

3. What lessons do you need to learn about forgiveness?

4. Use your journal to write about your inability to forgive. Be open and honest. It is a necessary part of being able to forgive.